Design
after
Dark

Thames and Hudson

Design

the story of

dancefloor

style

after

Dark

Cynthia Rose

Text copyright © **1991, Cynthia Rose**
Copyright © **1991, Thames and Hudson Ltd, London**
Reprinted in 1994

Designed by **Ian Swift**
Cover design by **Trevor Jackson**

Printed and bound in **Singapore**

To the memory
of
Jean-Michel Basquiat

December 22, 1960 – August 12, 1988

"Looking for art talent scouts? There are no art talent scouts.
Face it, no-one will seek you out."
Gary Panter
The Rozz-Tox Manifesto
April 1, 1980

During the latter half of the 1980s, London witnessed the
making of remarkable social history. From illicit radio stations
through improvised nightclubs, young Londoners helped to
construct a completely alternative leisure landscape. Its aim
was celebration, its glue was music and the changes it
engineered and explored now affect the music industry, the
advertising business and many related areas of design.
Socially, this world united Britons of many ages who differed
widely in background, race and taste. And the inspiration they
took from each other was broadcast across the globe.

This book is an attempt to look at their world through the visuals
it generated. I hope it captures at least a slice of the energy and
the events which shaped a fresh sense of possibility. Certainly it
cannot hope to capture all the names and faces involved: no
one book could contain the whole story. But as we near a new
century, the global outlook and visual joy of such designers,
artists, dancers and music makers should recharge us all.

Cynthia Rose

Contents

Introduction: A Social History

Profiles in Style: Eleven Dancefloor Designers

Dancefloor Revolution: The Roots

When young Britons took up Bolshevik design, they welcomed it into their wardrobes and set it to a beat

NIGHT; April 1985. Outside an underground station in West London, a growing crowd peers into the darkness. They are searching for the spray-painted signs which will guide them towards avant-pop group Test Department's "Greater London Council Farewell Gig". Administrator of community services for England's capital city, the GLC remains politically singular: although Mrs Thatcher's Tories run Britain, the GLC is Labour-controlled. And it has always carried a torch for the Do-It-Yourself ethic of England's late-70s punk movement: transforming derelict toilets into recording studios, funding a new city magazine (City Limits), supporting fringe arts bodies and mounting massive, regular music festivals.

Now it is to be abolished by the government. And with gigs like this one by Test Department, proponents of chic "industrial noise", thousands of young Londoners aim to protest. But these protesters also affirm:

London's infatuation with Russian revolutionary style pervades the diverse crowd. They come complete with belted coats, hammer-and-sickle badges, Dr. Zhivago hats, T-shirts emblazoned with Heroes of the People such as Marx, Lenin, cosmonaut Yuri Gagarin. Many have shaved their heads in the style of Bolshevik poet-designer Vladimir Mayakovsky (1893-1930).

Some are members of "Red Wedge", a "Left arts alliance" of young people who will work for Labour victory in the next General Election. Formed in early '85 with pop stars like Billy Bragg and Sade as supporters, Red Wedge takes its name from three sources. One is the "wedge" haircut - a smart look sported by officeworkers, football fans, jazz buffs and soul boys alike. The others? A Russian propaganda poster ("Beat the Whites With a Red Wedge") by El Lissitzky and a 1919 street installation by Nicolai Kolli.

As hundreds of punters converge on Test Department's performance site (a giant, abandoned railway roundhouse beneath a grubby flyover), most resemble young Muscovites of 1917 more than inhabitants of Ladbroke Grove, Stoke Newington or Southwark. Their D-I-Y Bolshevism is the cutting edge of street-style. And the buzz which fuels this crowd is palpable - it recalls the excitement of "secret" punk gigs almost a decade before.

Above: Neville Brody's logo for left-wing arts alliance Red Wedge

Pop groups like Crass and Test Department had political aims. To publicise them, they turned to an old political tool: the handbill. Often this was the only advertisement for their aims

10

CITY LIMITS

LONDON'S POLITICS ★ ART ★ CINEMA ★ MUSIC ★ THEATRE

SILENT MOVIES TO CIVIL WAR

TINA MODOTTI:

MARCH 26 TO APRIL 1 1982 NO.25. 50P

In 1981, the former staff of London listings weekly Time Out launched a new magazine of their own. They called this competitor City Limits, and its format was set by designer David King. King continued for some time to contribute weekly covers.

Above: record sleeves from the Rocking Russian design collective helped exploit a post-punk taste for Soviet style (left). But with work for bands like the Scars (right), they anticipated a less Eurocentric vision

Which is hardly surprising; UK pop culture's fascination with Soviet style and design has endured for almost ten full years. What seems a fluke of fashion is, like these punters, merely surfacing after a long, subterranean journey. And in the five years which follow this evening, young Londoners with little more than style in common will alter British aesthetics. They will come to grasp imagery as an international language - one whose vocabulary can bridge cultural differences.

While mainstream pundits argue over a culture they claim is reduced to codes of consumption, these young Britons will succeed in staging a dancefloor revolution. It will not be the Komsomol-style overthrow dreamt of tonight by Red Wedge. Instead, it will come about through grass-roots changes - successive waves of guerilla sounds, guerilla design, guerilla entertainments. The new design dynamic will be an impulse born out of celebration, rising out of leisure enacted as event. And it will change young people's perceptions about what entities like design and communication should do.

Above all, this strange configuration of changes will bring young Britons a global perspective. It will inspire them to aim for an international future; one with unity and clarity for all. And their re-energised eyes will see. As designer Allan Parker put it in 1990:

Three Kliks' promo-video for Iggy Pop

" If you know how to read the images, if you listen to the real soundtrack, you can now travel around the world and catch what's going on. You can see a poster from Eastern Europe and know what frame of mind they're in. You can walk into an African club for an hour and understand the vibe. You can spend a week in Bombay and realise the energy there is such that in 10 years they'll eat our mainstream culture alive."

But in 1985, the mid-point of the decade, all this is yet to come. Instead, an old revolution is proving the strange tenacity of its art and symbols.

Russian images had surfaced on shirts designed by London punk collectives like Seditionaries, Boy and Fifth Column back in 1976. And an art student named Al McDowell took a summer job printing some of them. When McDowell found himself without a job, he turned to designing on his own - and called his studio Rocking Russian. "We were printing these shirts for the Sex Pistols. And one day in the Daily Mail a housewife wrote in and said, 'Whoever makes these shirts must be Russians!' It was perfect."

Rocking Russian diversified into State Arts (a T-shirt company responsible for importing the French "Fuck Art - Let's Danse" slogan onto British shores), a video production unit called Three Kliks, Grabuge magazine, and Direct Hit Records (which handled everything for its

Above: prophetically, i-D magazine represented the alliance of a streetwise designer, a nightclub habitue and Terry Jones, ex-Art Director of Vogue. Ten years later, Jones' book Instant Design (above, lower right) would demonstrate the importance of i-D's innovations

clients: management, fan club, design and press relations). Inspired by the Parisian punk design team Bazooka, McDowell's collective attracted a varied clientele of artisans. One of the most enthusiastic was recent art-school graduate Neville Brody.

In the summer of 1980, McDowell was persuaded by mainstream graphic designer Terry Jones (from '72 through '77 the Art Director of Vogue) to help found a magazine about street style - one they decided to call i-D. Retailing at 50p for 36 black-and-white pages stapled between covers of fluorescent card, i-D treated pop design as a matter of personal British creativity. It consisted mostly of reportage: kids stopped on the street, photographed, then asked about their dress and their personal associations.

i-D's third co-Editor was a nightclubber named Perry Haines; other contributors were Hell's Angels and ex-convicts. Sandwiched between the launches of The Face (in May 1980) and Blitz (in September 1980), their idiosyncratic "fashion directory" would typify young self-expression as lifestyle and - within five years - as an important British export. All the style mags nurtured struggling graphic, photographic and journalistic talents. But for art students and nightclubbers, i-D became the paper of record.

i-D was launched with punk design as well as punk principles. It employed the collage, street-level Situationism and graphic improvisation for which Sex Pistols design guru Jamie Reid had proselytized. And that choice proved prescient: today, affinities for these

practices continue to constitute a substantial chunk of young Britain's artistic unconscious.

Yet so does the romance with "Soviet style" - an underground impulse with equally uncanny resilience. And during the early '80s, a series of linked events kept Bolshevism as vision in front of the public eye.

David King, Art Editor of the Sunday Times magazine from 1965 to 1975, and designer extraordinaire of book jackets and political posters, was inspired by turn-of-the-century Russian graphics: over two decades, he had assembled a personal archive of Revolutionary photos, posters, handbills and ephemera.

King-designed catalogues for exhibitions such as the Oxford Museum of Modern Art's Mayakovsky: 20 Years of Work (1982) or the Crafts Council's 1983 Art Into Production, as well as his design of books like New Worlds: Russian Art and Society 1900-1937 (1986) and Trotsky (1987, 1991) helped to provide the impetus for an Anglo-Soviet graphic style. Even more widely seen was King's work for the Anti-Nazi League, Anti-Apartheid and his early cover designs for the London weekly City Limits, launched in 1981.

City Limits suffered from understaffing, limited resources and low-quality newsprint, but King's format tried to treat such handicaps as assets. His thick black bars, heavy type and expressionistic use of photographs (which he would screen heavily, crop inventively and generally exploit) incorporated the ingenuity of punk. Yet his graphic boldness and grasp of the overall project - the magazine as an

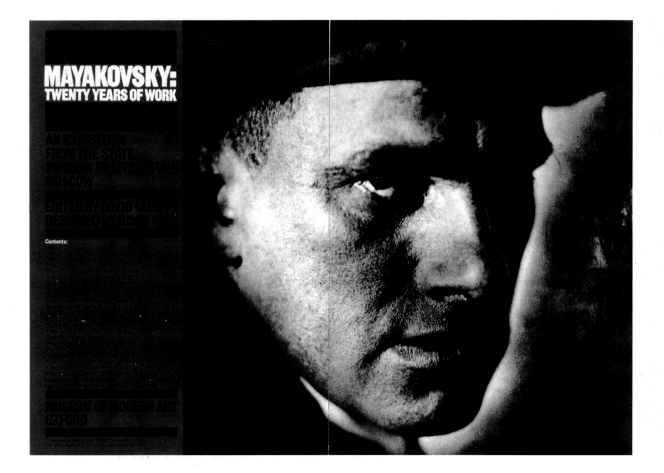

MAYAKOVSKY: TWENTY YEARS OF WORK

AN EXHIBITION FROM THE STATE MUSEUM OF LITERATURE MOSCOW

EDITED BY DAVID ELLIOTT DESIGNED BY

Contents:

MUSEUM OF MODERN ART OXFORD

Mayakovsky (above and below centre) became a pop-cultural idol. He sparked exhibitions (above), fashion (like the badge below right), and design (Rocking Russian stationery, below left)

Graphics guru David King (far left) was famous for his serious study of Russian history, as well as his own work. His efforts (like the Mayakovsky exhibition catalogue, opposite page, top) helped popularise it. So did London screenings of Russian revolutionary film (left, a British Film Institute video cover) and Warren Beatty's epic Reds (below)

individually distinct but weekly agitprop artefact - derived directly from Bolshevik mentors.

David King sees clear reasons why Soviet style should fascinate successive waves of young British talent. "Designers there had problems similar to those of students here: lack of money and lack of really good printing facilities. Stylistic technique at the time of the Revolution evolved from those conditions. The vision of that time demanded a new art. . . . But few of the young designers that art seduces have any grasp of the political history behind it."

In 1983, a season of Early Soviet Cinema at the National Film Theatre helped to keep Britons aware of the idealism that drove the original Bolshevik vision. 1984 and 1991, Paris couturier Jean-Paul Gaultier (who regularly admits his debt to British street style), unveiled "Russian Collections". In 1985, a student who had attended the first Gaultier show applied for work at London's Collett's International Bookstore, specialists in Russian-language books and "world literature". In his job interview, Matthew Gibson claimed he could make an agitprop T-shirt and apparel department pay.

Commissioning designs by artists he knew or admired, Gibson brought the underground sensibility upfront in a matter of months. Courier bikers quartered in a square behind the shop gave his Soviet shirts free, city-wide publicity. Sales boomed, more designs were needed - and young Britons formed design teams with titles like MAX, Marks and Stalin, CCCP, SMASH, Seeing Red. Through an obligingly snowbound winter, the craze for Anglo-Russian graphics and fashion flourished. It even earned a scathing nickname: "designer socialism". In 1986, one-time Rocking Russian employee (now Face Art Director) Neville Brody re-designed New Socialist magazine, and many felt that the graphic flair he brought to this task redeemed the epithet. Certainly, it lent the movement wider currency.

Neville Brody succeeded in marrying style to politics. He caught the basic impulse of young Anglo-Russian romance, the fascination David King believed to be superficial. Yet Brody was not the only style-monger fuelled by Russian panache. It was just as important to Terry Jones, who trained at Good Housekeeping and Vanity Fair before co-founding i-D. "I had been influenced by Russian Constructivist design and wanted the conflict of black bars across halftone images," remembered Jones in 1990. "Although far from revolutionary, when I ran the information crawler through the middle of the TV image on 01 For London - in 1987 - we still got complaints."

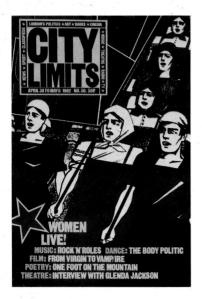

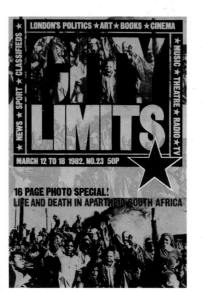

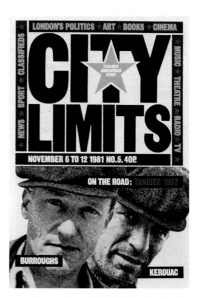

The impact of David King's weekly covers
for City Limits did not depend upon cash,
extensive research or even a good photo.
His real tools were boldness, imagination
and a grasp of the focus in each issue

POP

"FUCK ART LET'S DANSE"

Ten years after Rocking Russian's legendary Fuck Art - Let's Danse T-shirt (itself a slogan pirated from France), KISS-FM's "Free" magazine carried an ad for a new shirt bearing the same slogan, by London designer Graham Joyce

Event: The New Community

As the 1980s progressed, so did the design of those handouts which advertised London clubs and "raves". Top: Wetworld; centre: Habit; bottom: High On Hope

It was music which translated the visuals into theatre, and music which would spark a change in the very nature of youthful British leisure

The crowds massing for Test Department in 1985 carry in their perceptions as well as on their chests two British design sensibilities: punk serendipity and classicism, Bolshevik-style. At the concert, they are destined to encounter a third: a different undercurrent which, over the next five years, will build and build until it too transforms design and leisure. Discovering its genesis is as simple as stepping through the door of that derelict railway roundhouse.

There, within the hulking iron structure, over a thousand punters mingle shoulder to shoulder in the Easter chill. Some inspect the specially designed banners - 30' tall - at the back of the circular hall. Others contemplate a 40' slogan ("THE UNACCEPTABLE FACE OF FREEDOM") which decorates one centre-stage column. The stage itself rises ten feet above the centre of the building's floor: a circle within the iron circle of the bizarre venue itself.

Test department design for flyers and T-shirts

This stage is strewn with sculptures by Malcolm Poynter, and by West London's Mutoid Waste collective. They are made with panels, barrels, coils, and huge chunks of industrial junk metal; plus assorted ropes, red banners, microphone stands and heavy rope nets. When the lights flare up onstage, they reveal a lone bagpiper.

His pipes begin to keen - and nine synchronised film projectors programmed by Brett Turnbull and the Housewatch team (George Saxon and Alison Winkle) swing simultaneously into action. They flood the huge, enclosing walls with constantly changing images from the nation's psyche and press: headlines, striking miners, Maggie Thatcher and Lady Di. Then Test Department themselves stride onstage, in black Bolshevik-model trousers and spanking-white T-shirts. They begin to pummel and pound their industrial-strength percussion devices, slamming over-amplified drum pedals into rusted-out, 500-gallon steel tanks. Against each wall, between the glimmering projections and the crowd, a phalanx of dancers perform in Socialist-Futurist costume (alternatively white and black, as they switch shifts).

Onstage in the centre, a bare-chested black male dancer spins a huge, red silk flag, which gives way to a militant miner declaiming a lengthy

JUSTICE

Left and below: with energy, choreography and sheer noise, Test Department milked the excitement of combining crowds with a sense of spectacle and purpose

Initially, leisure-as-event was a matter of improvisation: put together with what was to hand. At West London's Mutoid Waste Company raves (left), the name of the game was "creative salvage"

poem. As the ensemble's seamless drive builds, taped music underscores the whole extravaganza, bouncing off the metal walls. The force becomes something seismic. And for almost an hour, the pace never flags; the choreography seems perfect. Things end with a crescendo of sound, steam and sweat flying into the stage lights - while two aerialists in flaming red bodysuits spin on ropes above the crowd. (deluxe magazine, summer 1985)

This spectacle is breathtaking but uncanny. It is exactly like the collaborations of Meyerhold and Mayakovsky - yet also completely British, as it translates a social moment into hyperbolic theatre. Afterwards, in a bar improvised from planks and scaffolding, a member of Test Department confides that the budget for two evenings of such histrionics has amounted to over £100,000. To help make up the cost, The GLC Farewell Gig will be taken on the road to Berlin.

Test Department's performance was a seminal and spectacular example of the form - leisure as event - which will alter UK youth culture, style and design in the late 1980s. Such events will take many forms: the one-off nightclub, the warehouse party, the two-step house party, reggae "blues", acid house "do", performance piece or "orbital rave". But, always, music is the central, animating principle: a means for bringing together young people of different races and tastes - a way to fire imaginations and inspire kids to create for themselves. That inspiration will go hand-in-hand with changes in film, recording technologies, dress and advertising. And all of them will depend on fresh strategies in design.

Most of these 1980s "raves" were organised and supervised by loose affiliations of young Britons formed into crews, posses or partnerships. Their names are deliberately flamboyant and evocative: The Mutoid

Waste Company, Westworld, Family Funktion, Shake 'N' Fingerpop, General Practice, Coldcut, Soul II Soul, Starship Enterprises. They stage some events to make money, some to have fun, others to publicise ventures which range from clothing designs to illegal radio stations and political causes. But, music being the common factor, most such events are commanded by their presiding DJs, those young men and women who supervise the sound. Or as black Britons put it - those who carry the swing.

In Britain's West Indian communities, DJs - and "MCs" and "toasters" - have always been the ruling personalities of the sound systems (large, mobile discotheques run as businesses, often by families). But as English youth culture changed in the '80s, multicultural schools were augmented by leisure exposure to new social customs and in particular to black aesthetics. Midway through the decade, this process accelerated because of the pirate radio boom.

Although not confined to London, this '80s pirate phenomenon presented capital-dwellers with 30 to 40 stations which daily merchandised music, humour and slang from across the black diaspora. (That is to say, reggae, soul and hip-hop, enhanced by underground news and chat rather than the ersatz "personality" of commercial radio.)

Pirate stations made their DJs into new British folk stars: underground, illicit voices sweetening the urban air. Irrespective of race or age, anyone could tune in every time they hit the airwaves. They played the music - black music - British youth wanted to hear but were denied by official outlets. Such stations remained one step ahead of the government sound police; after a bust, they took particular pride in quickly reclaiming the airwaves. But their Situationist aura also came from the kind of sounds they played: the things black (later "dance") music was doing by the late 1980s.

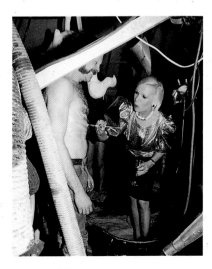

Raves were the evening face of a culture undergoing change – a Britain warming up to street life and cross-cultural interactions. The scenes taking place in its clubs, pubs and performance spaces were recorded in work by young artists such as Fiona Hawthorne (above). Left: a more theatrical view of communality at a Mutoid Waste Company party

Situationists of Style

The tools of dancefloor disc jockeys brought back punk subversion, changing design as well as sound

Situationism, understood by art students as the use of urban landscape and its contents to subvert (or antagonise) the established order, ruled the best-selling graphics of punk. And their fame was reprised periodically during the 1980s. In 1985, there was a Mayfair exhibit of Jamie Reid's work; in 1987, the publication of Up They Rise (designed by Reid and Assorted Images' Malcolm Garrett); and in 1989 the publication of Greil Marcus' 431-page book Lipstick Traces - plus a Situationist Internationale Fortnight at London's ICA. Yet what spurred the late-'80s renaissance of real Situationist practice in Britain was sound and not theory.

That sound, widely disseminated over the illegal airwaves, was the playful and immediate art of the club DJ - an art whose design depended upon several constituents. There was mixing: the dancefloor art of melding separate records into a single stream of continuous sound. Then there was scratching: manipulation of the needle in the vinyl groove, creating sound at once part of and different from the recording. There was digital sampling: electronic poaching of already-recorded sounds, "beats and breaks", to make up entirely separate tunes. Then, there was re-mixing - the DJ's use of all these techniques, to create consecutive versions of the same song. As Gene Santoro wrote in the American weekly The Nation:

DJs who work turntables replace bands as sound sources. Left out of the high-priced music wars by their lack of access to sophisticated equipment, the early 1970s black street musicians, like their graffiti-artist contemporaries, re-shaped a form by using what was cheap and available: turntables, old records, manual dexterity. They molded shredded musical history into new shapes within a single tune. (June 25, 1990)

The freedom and challenge of thus personalising a sound was not lost on young Britons - nor was the simplicity of the skills involved. By 1987, Britain's Amstrad computer company was running frequent TV ads for a budget "home mixing system". The same year saw the release of an LP called "1987, What The Fuck Is Going On?" by Bill Drummond and Jimmy Cauty, aka "The Jams" or "The Justified Ancients of Mu Mu". The Jams' album was released by the duo's label - an enterprise calling itself KLF: the Kopyright Liberation Front.

The Jams' record approached mainstream rock music the way hip-hop approached soul history, cutting and pasting to invent new

The "incomplete works" of punk graphic star Jamie Reid were carried on by a new generation. But the Technics turntable became their tool

From a squat in South London to Number One in the national charts? For the prankish partnership KLF (seen far left and below), by 1991 it had happened not once but three times. Home technology carried these non-musicians into video, television, even live performance

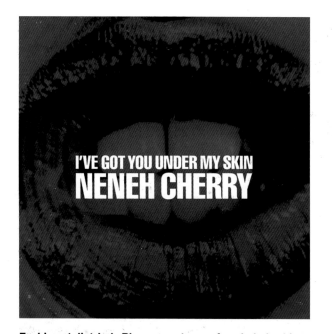

Fashion stylist Judy Blame, a veteran of punk, helps big-league pop names learn to mix visually. Above: Blame colleague Neneh Cherry scrambles Cole Porter, sexual politics and rap; below: Blame graphics for Massive Attack, extrapolated from the symbols on toilets

versions of classics that ranged from the Beatles' "All You Need Is Love" to Dave Brubeck's "Take Five". But not everyone got behind the idea of freeing their copyrights. Abba, the mega-successful Swedish popsters, threatened KLF with a lawsuit over the use of samples from their track "Dancing Queen". Only weeks after its release, "1987, What the Fuck Is Going On?" was withdrawn from distribution.

The might of pop monoliths, however, could not halt the march of kopyright liberation. The Jams went on in many guises: The Timelords, Disco 2000, Rockman Rock and Kingboy D, The KLF, The Orb. As The Timelords in 1988, their single "Doctorin' The Tardis" scored a pop No. 1, sparking off another controversy with its "allusions" to long-running BBC series Doctor Who. This time, the sampling bandits won. Though deluged with threats from BBC lawyers, The Timelords performed their national hit on BBC-TV's Top of the Pops. Worldwide, the record sold over a million copies.

By 1990, the bedroom mixers had taken control. A kid who called himself "Dave Angel" walked into RCA Records, bearing his homemade remix of a tune by the Eurythmics' Annie Lennox. Faced with paying up or "hearing it anyway", RCA unwillingly backed a record made for nothing in his Walthamstow bedroom. That summer, visiting folk star Suzanne Vega used newspaper interviews to plead for a meeting with remixers who called themselves "DNA". A DNA mix of her acoustic tune "Tom's Diner" had taken it into the national Top Ten. "They bootlegged it," Vega complained to Adam Porter of London's Evening Standard. "Then my record company decided to put it out . . . I only like cover versions if they pay."

British youth carried the inspirations of mixology into every sphere. From leather jackets to rubberwear, young designers "customised" clothing and called it a whole new look: Creative Salvage, Economy Ecology, "Trash Fashion". Stylists added garbage off the streets to fashion spreads. Graphic artists, too, felt free to pillage and mix their styles. For the hippest constituent of the DJ arts was homage to the immediate. And their most subversive quality was the irrepressible urge to find a new use for the Same Old Things.

Mix records also made a virtue of density; they packed even seconds of music with layers of reference and sound. That leap into three dimensions was one many designers soon tried to emulate: John England and Graham Elliott, for example, who met at the Royal College of Art in May 1987, designed RCA's cover for Dave Angel's Eurythmics remix in 1990. Their first project together was the decor for a college ball. True to the moment, they envisioned it as pure event rather than just music with art. "First of all," says England, "we filled the canteen with sand. Then we built sets and costumes. Our idea was a 'time warp' - a soundtrack journey between different eras."

Elliott describes a horse "which turned into a galleon. Then into a giant spaceship. Then we had a desert island with a creature inside which broke open."

In short, it was musical theatre: club art for the '80s. A tutor who attended the ball sponsored the duo to mount another (called

Bedroom mixers did what they wanted with sound from the famous as well as the obscure. And designers were intrigued by the challenge of a visual equivalent. Left: Living Colour LP sleeve by the Thunderjockeys; right: their sleeve for an illicit Eurythmics remix further altered by M/A/R/R/S DJ Dave Dorrell

Spectacle Yummy Yummy) in Holland. Elliott graduated in June, and work with the younger England appeared in his degree show. It was seen by Edward Booth-Clibborn, of Design & Art Direction, who invited Elliott and England to New York - as a team. Calling themselves the Thunderjockeys, they set off with 100 slides ("remixed images of desire") and a sculpture "covered in pink fur, with collapsible whirring bits".

The trip to New York netted the Thunderjockeys clients like CBS Records and brought them respect in the world of commercial design. In 1989, the "TJs" designed D & AD's annual European Illustration. And, in between, they have worked on sleeve art, adverts, MTV "art breaks" (Thunderwear, Thunderjockeys in Outer Space), videos, and a number of massive theatrical parties. Explosive and electric, their work marries hard and soft, naivete and sophistication, control and effusive anarchy. In short, they became graphic re-mixers.

Thunderjockey sleeves for bands like Living Colour and the Todd Terry Project complement state-of-the-genre sound with joyously updated art. They also offer proof that computers can be as streetwise as the mixing console. "We use computers just like we would pick up a pencil or hammer," says John England. "They're just a tool. We've worked on Apples, on Scitex, with the Quantel Paintbox. But we don't possess a

computer of our own. We rent the time at facility houses, just like anyone else."

The Thunderjockeys typify that dancefloor design which specialises in barrier-busting, yet places more importance on inventiveness than on budget. From Chris Sullivan's Cubistic murals for the Wag Club in '83 through that recycled refuse with which the "Muties" adorned their late-'80s warehouse events, such design replaced lavish spending with lateral thinking. And, even with mainstream clients, the Thunderjockeys try to apply the same style of intrepid improvisation. "People worry too much about their parameters," says Elliott. "They say, 'There's only this money - we have to use cheap photographers, we have to use cheap type.' You should start with what you want; then find out how to do it. Go in and grab those new technologies by the balls!"

As with other young talents of the '80s (fashion-makers Chris Nemeth and Judy Blame, sound system Soul II Soul), initial commercial interest in this approach came from abroad. According to John England, "America took us seriously; there people fight to be first in taking a risk. Neville Brody talked a lot about deconstruction, about using graphics to break things down. But in Britain it doesn't happen like that. You have to force your way in."

Then & Now
The Style Files

From stapled chapbook to staid monthly; in its first decade of existence, i-D magazine altered Britain's discussion of young creativity. It started by reporting on kids who saw themselves as outsiders, ignored or at least marginal to the UK's creative professions. Then, along with its compatriots The Face and Blitz, it took their tastes seriously – and continued to explore them.

In doing this, i–D used one graphic trick which betokened its change of perspective. It took the format of that most upscale project, the woman's magazine fashion shoot, and imposed it upon snapshots from Britain's clubs and streets. In conventional fashion layouts the "details" of clothing choices, prices and stockists are relegated to corners and small print. But in i-D, as the

i-D!

STRAIGHT UP

Photographed by Steve Johnston

3 COLIN: Mode - Colin is wearing black pleated trousers which he made himself. The cardigan is from Marks and Spencers, £9.99 and the shoes from Axiom in the Kings Road, £5.99. Fave music - Siouxsie and the Banshees and David Bowie.

Anonymous girl with spiky hair-do.

6 MINNIE: Mode-J'kt,Warehouse-£8.99. "I bought it because it was cheap".T'rs from BOY,Kings R'd-£17.00.Music;"I use to be into the Mod revival stuff,now I hate it.It's just clinging on-to something to follow".And now?"I love Carlos Santana,my boyfreind plays his albums all the time" On Fashion-I Holidayed in New York and England-a far more developed Fashion Culture.I chose clothes that suit me rather than follow trends-......................."I like the way my boyfreind dresses,he wears those big,big padded shoulders-the Art School style")...........

PENNIE: Mode-J'kt-Cardiff.Skirt,"I'ts from Top Shop and I shortened it my self". Jumper,"I got it from some shop in Oxford s't,I can't remember the name.i get so mesmerized when I shop along Oxford S't.I never notice the names),Shoes.They are from Ravel.I can't remember how much.No doubt more th,n thy are worth.Pennie plays with th body snatchers.(Naughty girl.E.d.)......................

Alison.
1st Year Student,
Philosophy,
University of Sussex.
Leather jacket from
<u>Leather shop</u>,
Norwich:
£25.00
Skirt borrowed from
<u>Welsh friend</u> living
in Amsterdam:
No charge
Leggings made from
pieces of material
picked up in
<u>jumble sale</u>:
75p
T-shirt from <u>Nepal</u>:
about 10 rupees
Earring borrowed
from <u>friend at</u>
<u>Manchester Poly</u>:
No charge
Shoes from <u>Army</u>
<u>Surplus</u>, Newcastle:
£12.00
Rings from <u>Greece</u>
<u>and France</u>:
10 Drachmas/6 Francs
Bangles bought in
<u>Spain and India</u>:
*can't remember the
price but very cheap*
Cash provided
by savings
made with
<u>Young Person's</u>
<u>Coach Card</u>:
*£5.00
valid for 12 months*
Fares:
*Lower than other
forms of transport*
<u>Discount</u> allowed:
*About 30% on National
Express and Caledonian
Express services*
<u>Availability</u>:
*Any National Express
agent, Student Travel
Office or send off coupon.*

Daniel.
3rd Year Student
Anthropology
Sussex University.
Leather jacket from
<u>unknown shop</u>
in Colchester:
£40.00
T-shirt bought
in <u>China</u>:
12 Yuang
Trousers from
<u>unknown shop</u>
in Chelmsford:
£15.00
Boots from
<u>Army Surplus</u>
store Norwich:
About £10.00
Bangles bartered
for in <u>Thailand</u>
<u>China and Nepal</u>.
Belt from
<u>unknown shop</u>
in Norwich:
About £10.00
Hair set and
hennaed by
<u>Daniel</u> himself:
No charge
Cash provided
by savings
made with
<u>Young Person's</u>
<u>Coach Card</u>:
*£5.00
valid for 12 months*
Fares:
*Lower than other
forms of transport*
<u>Discount</u> allowed:
*About 30% on National
Express and Caledonian
Express services*
<u>Availability</u>:
*Any National Express
agent, Student Travel
Office or send off coupon.*

Send to National Express, FREEPOST, Box 145, Birmingham B11 2AF. Make cheque or P.O. payable to National Express Ltd. Please allow 14 days for delivery. You will need a passport sized photo to fix to the card on receipt. (No postage stamp required.)

NAME _____

ADDRESS _____

_____ POSTCODE _____

DATE OF BIRTH _____ I certify that I am between 16 and 23

SIGNATURE _____ TF/31/8

DISCOUNT COACH CARD »

Lower fares • The Cheapest Travel Card • 30% discount

layout trumpeted, they were the heart of the matter. "Interesting things come out of accidents," said co-Editor Al McDowell at the time of i-D's first issue."From putting opposing things together."
"A whole lot of things about fashion really switch me off ," he added. "People in that industry rely so much on what they're told. Style really comes down to a person's own presence. And that's more to do with how they FEEL they look."

Opposite page: 1980 layouts from Issue One of i-D. Left: what the style bibles launched, others learned to exploit. This ad, which was one in a series for Discount Coach Cards, appeared in 1990

Portable Art and All That Jazz

Dancefloor art was transient because clubs were staged only once a week or, sometimes, only once. Yet their art engendered a feeling of excitement and community

In nightclubs, art was ephemeral. But it catalysed new trends and a whole new brand of British optimism

Pirate radio gave regular, constant reinforcement to young peoples' determination to be heard and seen. When the stations staged clubs, contests and phone-ins to publicise themselves, their listeners eagerly played a part. They also devoured the handbills, bulletins, T-shirts and baseball caps designed to promote competing stations. By the autumn of

Handbill image by Andrea Diamond

1989, the pirates' popularity was so overwhelming, their individual station profiles so high, and the advertising they sold so successful in reaching a new leisure market, it forced actual changes in British broadcasting law. In 1990, pirates such as Bristol's FTP ("For The People") and London's Kiss-FM won a right to legal existence. Things had been "broken down".

A parallel to the pirates was the capital's array of club nights: colourful, one-off affairs held in venues rented night by night. Such clubs boasted evocative titles - The Payback, The Dirtbox, The Wherehouse, Dr D's Rhythm Miracle, RAW, Delirium, The Bunker, The Sweatbox, Centre of the World. They were publicised by cheaply printed flyers or "tickets", and emphasised portable decor: banners, slides, drapes, posters, wall-projected films. Once a club night made money, it could become a weekly fixture on the scene. And when it came to more secretive, entertainment-intensive events, young club-runners quickly learned to exploit the pirate stations. On-air publicity was less demanding (and less traceable) than even flyers.

Pirate stations proved ideal for hyping the big "warehouse parties" which sprang up during 1985: black and white and Asian Londoners joining to stage illicit jams in the bowels of derelict buildings. Initiated to make money (a fiver was paid at the door and a few cases of beer would provide an impromptu bar), the "warehouse" went on to do much more.

"Warehouse raves brought together a new crowd," says DJ Jazzie B, whose black Soul II Soul crew from North London was one of the first to join forces with young white entrepreneurs. "Because young people checked it as a form of rebelling. And the music you gave them had to be brilliant. 'Cause these were just old buildings where you'd kicked in the

Increasingly, the dancefloor was where Britain's real young movers and shakers went to express fashion, slogans, graphics, humour, new grooves and sharp moves

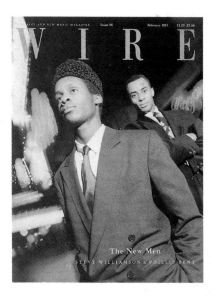
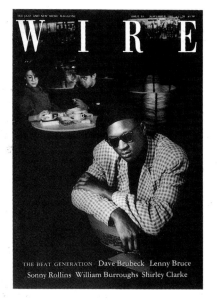
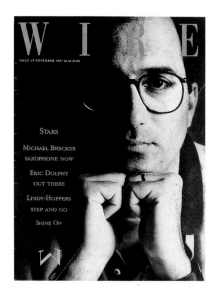

Above: the jazz magazine Wire, once
a bastion of academic purism,
achieved a cult status with both
clubbers and designers under the
art direction of Paul Elliman

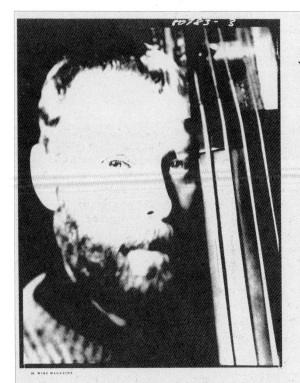

STILL LIFE
WITH BASS
AND CELLO

DAVE HOLLAND
IN PURSUIT OF
THE CUBIST BASS
LINE BY GRAHAM
LOCK | PHOTO
NICK WHITE

1. COLOUR
IN 1971 Dave Holland said, "timbre has been the most
important development in modern music".
In 1988 I ask him, why?
"Hmm. At that time I was looking beyond the notes
themselves to the attack and timbre you gave them. How a
note was treated in terms of sustain, vibrato, the kind of
texture you gave a note, the colour – these seemed very
expressive qualities to me.
"I think more recently my attention has been on rhythmic
development in the music, and right now I'm most interested
in resolution – the way the rhythm resolves, the harmony
resolves. You know how you go along listening to music . . . I
call it selective listening. It's like when you look at paintings.
Until somebody points out to you the dimension of colour,

say, you don't really see what's happening with the yellow and
the red and so on. Then suddenly your eyes are opened. It's the
same with music.
"My attention is on resolution now, and when I go back and
listen to Charlie Parker's records, or Coltrane's, I'm hearing a
lot of new things because I'm listening to that particular
element in a more exact way.

2. PERSPECTIVE
HE SITS on the hotel-room bed, an amiable, articulate
man, not looking his 41 years. If such things mattered, you
could describe him as one of England's premier musicians
(though he has lived in America since 1968); a bassist and
cellist renowned worldwide for a technique that allows him
incredible speed and facility, yet without losing the sensitive,

46 WIRE MAGAZINE

WIRE MAGAZINE 47

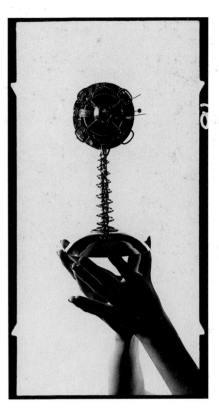

Left: Fiona Hawthorne's paintings and portraiture often graced Wire. Above, centre: Michael DeNardo's Wire Jazz Award statuette

door and wired things up. There would always be trash all over the floors, water everywhere, and only two or three lights."

A million miles from Test Department's big-budget project held the same year. But kin to it - and descended from the "New Romantic" and Gothic nightclubs (Blitz, Billy's, the Batcave) of the early '80s with their predilection for costume, makeup, and fantasy. The difference was young black Britons . . . a population which had highly developed leisure traditions of its own. Pirate stations existed on the vinyl skills and knowledge of young black DJs. But there were also West End hip-hop evenings (like the Titanic Club's Language Lab), a pantheon of jazz-dance teams (often to be seen at the mainstream Wag Club), and a fresh, British jazz movement which started to build when sax player Courtney Pine founded his Abibi Arts alliance in April 1985.

As young black Britons brought their own aesthetic into dancefloor culture, the style press rewarded them with media visibility. Once relegated to the two-step soul and house party scenes of Britain's black suburbs, by the mid-'80s black style was ruling the heart of London club culture.

It affected leisure pursuits at almost every level: fashion, pop video, music and merchandising. But the acknowledgment of young black style as central in a changing society owes much to the late fashion editor Ray Petri (The Face, Arena). Petri coined the term "Buffalo" for his version of club and street chic. And Buffalo was more than an adjective. It became an actual collective of stylists, singers and designers – dancefloor-universe talents like singer Neneh Cherry and stylist Judy Blame (aka Chris Barnes).

"Buffalo was built on the club vibe, like a sound system," said Blame in May 1990. "Everything was flexible, everyone could put in ideas. That's why it suited people like me. . . But Ray was important for something bigger than Buffalo. And that was his use of strong, brilliant black men and women. It's worth saying that now because, as Britain progresses, that's what's really exciting. That's what sells around the world: our ragamuffin, hip-hop, multi-racial moment. Not just in music and style, but in life."

From 1985, Britain's new jazz also began to gain recognition. And it shaped a design vehicle of its own: a jazz magazine called The Wire.

Left: when Wire hosted Britain's 1987 National Jazz Awards, both publicity and event were aimed at young, club-conscious fans and creators of the new jazz

Opposite page, top: Judy Blame's "Dying Waters" fashion spread for the May 1980 issue of i-D, photographed by Jean Baptiste Mondino. For a decade, Blame's influential imagination has schooled young Britons in using trash with flash

**Left: Buffalo fashion
by the gifted stylist
and art director
Ray Petri; Petri's
genius redirected
men's fashion**

Purchased in 1984 by Quartet Books' proprietor Naim Atallah, The Wire (eventually, Wire) was edited by ex-New Musical Express staffer Richard Cook. It began life by maintaining the purist snobberies common to white British record collectors, and jazz buffs in particular. But under young designer Paul Elliman, who joined in 1985, Wire's visuals reflected a warmer, livelier, younger British scene. In graphic terms, Elliman gave the scene strict focus - a typographical rigour and austerity inspired by glossy American fashion mags of the 1940s and '50s.

This fastidious style-consciousness pleased Britain's young jazz snobs, most of whom were snappy dressers and fervent nightclub fans. By November 1987, when Wire staged Britain's National Jazz Awards, they did so at the tony Waldorf Hotel. And from invitations to posters and the award statuettes (surrealistic chrome microphones designed by sculptor/jeweller Michael DeNardo), the coherence of that package reflected de facto acceptance of young black British style.

Elliman's love of jazz combined with his own involvement in London's dancefloor underground to give Wire unexpected influence. As with i-D and The Face, graphic designers, photographers and art students often drifted into the magazine's office. Such visitors would usually find themselves given a chance to contribute. This belief in taking risks brought notice to work like Fiona Hawthorne's drawings and the portraiture of photographer Mark Lewis.

33

Fresh Technology & Rare Grooves

As clubs like Barrie Sharpe and Paul Anderson's The Cat in the Hat proliferated, they brought Dancefloor Justice to black DJs: men like Trevor Shakes (above)

By 1988, the expansion of Britain's black music scene prompted another, more "street-level" British jazz mag, Straight No Chaser. Chaser began that June as the private project of ex-New Musical Express Editor Neil Spencer, DJ/Wire columnist Paul Bradshaw and colleague Kathryn Willgress. All were primarily writers. But they wanted their magazine to be visually set apart from the Wire magazine.

Straight No Chaser was conceived to be completely written and designed on the Apple Mac computer. Its initial format was established by consortium, with former NME Art Editor Andy Martin finalising the input. But Chaser's visuals were mostly a matter of chance for over a year. Finally, its team took on Ian Swift. At that time, the end of 1989, Swift was a member of Neville Brody's studio. Since 1986, he had assisted Brody in designing The Face and in the founding of Arena magazine (1988). A pragmatic Northerner who grew up on Merseyside and studied the art which Manchester's Factory Records built, Swift embodied the views of a new generation.

Banner design by Soul II Soul's Derek Yates

"For the past decade," he says, "British pop and style design has really been this 'Big Three': Peter Saville of Factory Records, Malcolm Garrett of Assorted Images, and Neville Brody. But they've all moved on. In the late '80s, you're getting people who already took that in. We've got the last 10 years under our belts, but we've been subject to very different influences. Graphic design is now a lot looser. Events like rare groove and acid house are the things which shape our work."

Ian Swift trained on the Apple Mac, and uses it for all his work. But he doesn't use the technology to facilitate imitation or "homage". "The Russian thing is the best example: I took from that a spirit rather than literal shapes and styles. Before Brody and his colleagues, no one had really looked at early Russian typography. David King used it just as a starting point, he looked to the ideals. Then you got all these designers using bits of that past as ammunition - with which to compete among themselves."

The social and leisure changes of the past five years, says Swift, produced a different rationale. "Designers raised on the new technology have another approach. Whether it's Constructivism or Swiss typography, they don't just want to plunder the past. So you get a moment like rare groove, which involves replication. But young designers responding to that won't imitate -

The dancefloor revolution came about through grassroots changes: guerilla sounds, guerilla design, guerilla entertainments

By 1988, London street culture was driven by black style, and new magazines like Straight No Chaser (cover above by Andy Martin) exploited the change. So did flyers for gigs like 1987's massively attended reunion of James Brown's band (below)

Above: Trevor Jackson's sleeve for the re-issue of Carwash

Above: Andrea Diamond's designs gave a rare groove image

Above: record fairs sponsored by pirate radio stations helped circulate the sound of the drum and the bass on vinyl

Above: American black music from the 1970s used design to display its politics

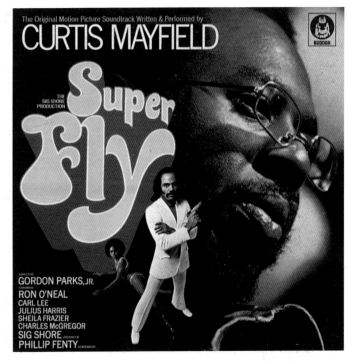

Above: vintage sounds and art inspired a new generation

Above: groups like London's Brand New Heavies rode the rare groove trend with a pastiche style. In the spring of 1988, they even released a fake import single whose Phantasy label parodied that of an early American independent, Fantasy Records

LWR's - BUST UP CREW
Wed 25th May 88

LWR
92.05 F.M.
Tel: 01-737 1344

ZIGI'S
225 STREATHAM HIGH ROAD, SW16
10.00p.m. till 2.00a.m.
ADMISSION: £1.50 (With this card)

DONT.
TALK ANY SHIT —
NO DRUG STORY'S
NO SEX OR SEXIST COMMEN
NO DRINK STORY'S MUSIC

DELIRIUM! MEMBERSHIP

OCEANS

VINYL LAB RECORDS
Presents

THE SHAFT
on
FRIDAY 27 MAY 1988
9.00pm - 2.00am

Musical Scene By
Sammy Sam
from Easy Chic
Spider P
From Rock To Rock
O'Bryan
from Vinyl Lab Records

P.A.'s - Power Cut
and
Average House Band

ADMISSION
£5.00

LIMITED TICKETS ONLY, Available from
Vinyl Lab Records . 58, Goldhawk Rd.
Shepherd's Bush W12 - Tel: 740 9881

Soul II Soul Shop
162, Camden High St.
NW1 - Tel: 262 3995

Quaff Records . 133, Stroud Green Rd.
London N4 - Tel: 272 3829

OCEANS
Acton Shopping Precinct
Acton High St. - Tel: 993 5888

Whether you called it a flyer, a ticket or a handout, this PR tool reflected the personal touch of pirate radio's many entrepreneurs. Above, centre: the sign in KISS-FM's secret broadcast studio. Surrounding it: club flyers, which could also double for "membership cards", and soon became the index of changing tastes in club sounds and fashions

DANCE WICKED
THURSDAY 26TH MAY

1200 PEOPLE WILL BE BACK ON
THE DANCE FLOOR OF THE

**ELECTRIC
BALLROOM**

CAMDEN TOWN NW1
LOOKING WICKED!

WILL YOU BE ONE OF THEM?

---

they'll interpret. They look to the spirit of the actual thing itself."

Rare groove, a London-based craze for the funk music and style of black America's '70s, exploded during the moment of pirate radio's greatest prominence. The term was a DJ catchphrase for exhumed soul records (Derek Boland's "good groove" on pirate station LWR became the "rare grooves" promoted by Norman Jay on KISS-FM). During 1986, such vinyl fetched astronomical prices in London shops and record fairs. But two things about "rare groove" proved even more influential.

One was the fact that this was Britain's first-ever black-driven musical fad: even Northern soul had been the province of white collectors. The other was the extent to which "rare groove" transformed the club scene, fusing fashion, sound and art the way it succeeded in fusing race. By the end of 1988, the '70s fad had even reached the high street. James Brown tapes were played in Miss Selfridge, and blue-jean manufacturers were planning the re-launch of flares.

Because record-collecting comprised the heart of the "rare groove" phenomenon, young designers were exposed to the florid, go-for-broke art on the sleeves of '70s LPs by James Brown and his coterie - as well as the highly prized soundtrack albums to films like Shaft and Carwash. Powerful product from artists such as Curtis Mayfield, Sly and the Family Stone, War, Donny Hathaway and Roy Ayers was constantly visible in shop windows, homes and clubs. And the message of such music - pan-Africanism and black pride - remained weightier than those platform shoes which also re-appeared. A new generation realised pop could comprise passions beyond those of Big Audio Dynamite or the Cult. And designers searched for new means by which to "express the vibe".

The design inspired by "rare groove" is not to be found on those official compilations ("Rare", "Rare Too", "Rare Soul", etc) with which record companies freed their '70's catalogues in hope of financial gain. It developed from flyers or "tickets". Handbills treated like mini-posters advertising gigs or clubs, tickets had always been a form of street publicity. They would be handed to punters leaving venues and left in stacks at record stores. For artists such as Andrea Diamond (whose bold, Matisse-like silhouettes gave the "rare groove" movement an unofficial logo), Mark Jackson (a xerox and graffiti artist), graphic designer Trevor Jackson, "Andy Art 21" and Chris Long (then a cartoonist), the ticket offered a cheap and portable space for constant experimentation.

Because they promoted one-off events, the average ticket became irrelevant after only a week. Yet flyers needed to grab the eye; they helped to build a venue or a club night's identity. With over forty clubs in action in London seven nights a week, the flyer scene was competitive. And, in the hands of late-'80s artists, this humble form of PR proved so successful that bookstores, fashion designers, even publishers, soon employed the same scheme.

The grooves were kept flowing on London's underground scene by salesmen like Kenrick Hurley (above left) and Lloyd "Daddy Bug" Brown (below left), who was known as the capital's "Cut-Out King"

Then & Now
Rare Groove Spins Off

Rare groove was a dancefloor phenomenon which touched unexpected nerves. By December of 1988, Afro-chic from the '70s had flooded London clubs, in the form of hip-hugging flares, Zodiac pendants, Afro wigs and belted leather coats.

The Duffer of St George boutique was promoting a Shaft or Superfly look; something intended to be worn at its counterpart club, The Cat In The Hat. Rare groove looked like just another of London's periodic fashion fads. But, as exponent Norman Jay maintained, there was more to the story. "It was 'OK: come to terms with the music of your day. Just let me show you where it came from, then it's not so transient.' The British collector mentality, rare groove changed all that. We showed things as inter-related, which no-one had been allowed to do before."

The lesson of interconnect-edness sank in, just as rare groove became an accepted term for a kind of music, like hip-hop or indie-pop. Three years later, on February 17, 1991, the Sunday Times magazine enthused about British fashion's "strongest collection in years". Its "secret" was funk – meaning flares, platform shoes, Afro wigs and Superfly-high stylistic exaggerations. And the designers were names long linked with an appropriation of street chic: Vivienne Westwood,

Rifat Ozbek, Katharine Hamnett and John Galliano.

Meanwhile, the soul underground itself had absorbed something more profound. Midway through 1988, the term "Afrocentric" was seldom heard. But, by 1990, British youth – black and white alike – knew from their clubs and turntables what it meant: pride, knowledge and unity among the black peoples of the world. This discovery fuelled an exploration of history which is only just beginning. And, where radio once promoted rare grooves, it now plays "Conscious Music": music which understands its past, which celebrates the links between separate lives and races and styles. And, for secondhand platform shoes, that's something of a legacy.

Academy Tickets £10.50 Academy Box office Tel 071 326 1022 and from usual agents (subject to booking fee) + support M.C. Mello PA by Jaye Ella Ruth + DJs Jasper, Vinyl Junkie, Dan Air / Film Ram / Jeff McCaxley / Jaz Nelson Fri 16th Nov / Sat 17th 9 - 3am Brixton

presents

The Return of the Funkateers
BOOTSY'S
RUBBER BAND
with the Horny Horns
FRED WESLEY & THE NEW J.B'S
featuring
MACEO PARKER & PEE WEE ELLIS

Above, centre: the first JBs Reunion gig sparked regular visits back to Britain by Brown's famous alumnae (flyer by Ian Swift). Below: a most unlikely fashion to spark social consciousness

A platform for debate

Once created, the underground marketplace rapidly expanded. Rare grooves gave way to "dance music", and fanzines like Soul Underground (below; 1987-1991) yielded to video magazines (right, Dance International)

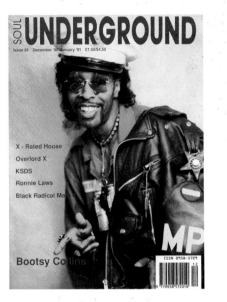

By 1990, even America was absorbing the message of rootsy Afrocentricity carried by UK artists like Caron Wheeler (below centre). The LP by Motown's Blaze (left) offered a deliberate pastiche of '70s reggae sleeves like those of Black Uhuru (above centre)

Behind The Scenes:
Sound System
Theory

Within the fellowship of turntables and dancefloors a new style of teamwork was changing British creativity

Nightlife led to business schemes which were an outgrowth of friendship (above, ticket for a warehouse party). This concept was designed into the Poizone clothing company's Circle of Friends logo

Designers like Diamond and Jackson were part of the nightlife their tickets advertised. Out at many a "rave", they sought to translate this leisure aesthetic and its language ("Dancefloor justice!") as both continued to evolve. And what they sought was a visual code which could communicate to other punters.

"Usually," Diamond recalls, "you wouldn't get more than a name and a few details. Or something like 'It should look rough.' But, as the scene expanded, design got a lot more competitive. Soon how your ticket looked was the guarantee - or not - of a quality rave."

What started with the warehouse party gathered unity through "rare groove" to create a mass British marketplace for "dance" (read black) musics. Continuing through musical movements like house and Acid House, it changed the leisure patterns of many young participants.

"Warehouses", says DJ Norman 'Original Rare Groove' Jay, "taught young Britons of different classes how to be social together outside the confines of work, clubs and football terraces. Taught them there didn't have to be rules - or expensive bars or doormen telling you what you could and couldn't wear. We freed people's imaginations."

And style was an integral part of such late-'80s changes. Attitude, dress and decor - however minimal - always remained central to the burgeoning dancefloor scene. Jay: "You always aimed to reflect the average young Briton's style-consciousness. It's the marriage of fashion, music and social concerns that makes London, in particular, unique. If the attitude of people who go to a club is bright and colourful - that makes for a brilliant night. . . . You could have all the records in the world. You could DJ brilliantly. But if the attitude isn't conducive, you're not gonna make it work."

Britain's "rare groove" movement also provided unorthodox business models - an impetus which succeeded where formal government schemes had failed. It schooled both promoters and punters in selling that slippery commodity, style. The proof of their expertise would arrive in 1989, with Soul II Soul's international sales success. But the phenomenon spawned by "rare groove" taught all its young entrepreneurs that - to quote Norman Jay - "business and creativity, personality and energy, need to work hand-in-hand."

"Anyone can engineer a hype," said Jazzie B in 1987. "But the only way to become successful is work until you deliver the goods." This was sound system theory; the rationale behind '70s mobile disco outfits like

What is "sound system theory"? Trevor Nelson: "It's business and commitment from a very early age. When you're young and you want a flash car and nice clothes, the only arena for that is the sound system. But it takes discipline. You work 9 to 5, then you DJ from some towerblock flat, then you work a rave all night with bags under your eyes. You carry your own boxes, do your own PR, buy your own records. But you can come out and DO BUSINESS. It may be a little unorthodox, but it works."

Reggae sound systems (left) gave rise to broader-based London "sounds" (right) in the mid-1980s

Sound systems trained pirate DJs (left, in 1981, KISS-FM's DJ Tee, Simon Goffe, Trevor Madhatter and Gordon Mac) and businessmen (right, in 1987, Soul II Soul's Jazzie B and HB)

London's Rapattack, Good Times, and Mastermind. Such systems were part of Britain's West Indian heritage; they derived from musical precursors in the Caribbean. And they were based around hard labour and bottom-line business sense as much as around turntable expertise. For sound system theory teaches that teamwork must be rooted in mutual esteem . . . in respect for the contributions and sweat and opinions of every participant.

As ravers apprehended it, sound system theory would change the creative orientation of many young Britons. It inspired them to found teams and partnerships and studios - instead of seeking just to exploit solo talent or personality. Absorbed indirectly, sound system theory has much to do with the birth of design teams like London's Creative Hands and the Thunderjockeys, Manchester's Central Station Design or Sheffield's Designers' Republic; styling collectives such as UTO, the "Unlimited Talent Organisation"; and organisations like Buffalo or Soul II Soul - in which sound and vision are equally central.

In 1987, Soul II Soul was a sound system involving a core of 16 plus satellites. Two of them, Derek Yates and Nicolai Bean, were designers. Yates produced a comic-book, History of Soul II Soul, as well as the "Funki Dred head": a portrait of Philip 'Daddae' Harvey which became the crew's logo. Nicolai Bean (aka Jennifer Lewis) had started as a graffiti artist. But by the late '80s, she had transferred that guerilla aesthetic into airbrushed shirt, waistcoat and jacket designs. These, like Yates's T-shirt designs, were sold in the London shop which Soul II Soul opened in November 1987 - a shop with an in-house DJ retailing vinyl alongside designer goods.

Bean evolved logos and portraits and banners for the crew's club nights, all aimed at giving the Soul II Soul experience a symbolic face. Many of her group portraits were updates of "rare groove" LP covers (like those by Earth, Wind and Fire). They rendered the sound system's frontmen in a style which could be called comic-book futurism. Derek Yates, who met Jazzie B through a mutual DJ friend, Kid Batchelor, approves of the Soul II Soul collective forging their own myth.

"You don't see many designers who deal with the world as it is," he says. "They either look to the past or they try to create some sort of ideal world - in opposition to reality." In 1987, Yates enrolled at Camberwell School of Arts & Crafts, "because when you operate out of a scene, your work can become derivative, which I wanted to avoid." But he retains his respect for a direct relationship - both with people and with the artefacts which communicate to them most clearly.

The comic-book, he says, is a good example. "Look at Jen's work, for instance, and you can tell she's looked at a lot of comics. Some designers I know would be very scornful of that. But they go too far in the other direction. They make work that is just obscure. Work without any real audience. I'm a great believer that art should please people." In the case of Jazzie B's posse, it did. As the fame of his crew's club nights grew (particularly after 1989, with the decision to start making records), they attracted young designers eager to work on banners, T-shirts - and the huge sculptures which featured in a weekly club night at South London's Fridge. In 1989, when they opened a second London shop, even the floor tiles and curtains were made by the crew's own designers. The mixture of

This page: for Soul II Soul, Derek Yates concentrated on pictures of communal endeavour. Opposite page: young design groups such as Manchester's Central Station (top: Happy Mondays sleeve) and London's Creative Hands (bottom left) pooled talents to further their joint aims

Above: collectives like the Unlimited
Talent Organisation ("UTO") or Buffalo
traded inspiration as well as credits

TRADITION

*... Artistic belief handed down
from one generation to another.*

DJ's	Fame ...
Trevor Madhatters	*(Borderline, Africa Center)*
Patrick Forge	*(Dingwalls, Fez)*
Marco	*(Wag)*
Mickey D	*(Black Market)*
Martin Madhatters	*(Dance Wicked)*
Fitzroy Buzzboy	*(Cask in the Glass)*
Eon Irving	*(Roof Garden)*

**Bank Holiday Sunday
August 26th 10pm - 5am**

at

The Arch,
66 Goding Street, Vauxhall SE11

Over 20's only

Funky Rasta

Back In Time

You Are In My System

Tell Me What To Do

Mysteries Of The World

Earthly Powers

Trouble Funk Express

The Bottle

The World Is A Ghetto

Fairplay

Glad You're In My Life

Dream Come True

Holdin' On

You're The One For Me

Party And Don't Worry About It

Funkin' For Jamaica

Dancing In Outer Space

Don't Tell It

Stoned To The Bone

In The Middle

**As club flyers like the one for Tradition (above right) show,
the new dancefloor paid its respects to the style, politics
and accomplishments of the sound systems and to those
artists who came before them. Top left: Virgo; bottom left:
Mastermind**

style, graphics and music defines Soul II Soul: for these young Britons, expressing oneself is a matter of sheer event.

And it is political. Jazzie B in 1987: "Style and dress and design are always very political. How you're taught to carry yourself affects you when you deal with the world. In this society, people make it or not for business reasons. But there's no-one in the world who should want to change who they are or how they feel. . . . To succeed you learn how to vet and streamline your own thing, make it communicate to the mass of people. You negotiate the business side: but only on your own terms." Your vision is important, says that world he helped young Britons to build: and your vision is what counts.

Even an artist and designer such as Fiona Hawthorne, who draws from life and is part of no studio, cites the sound system ethic of collective purpose as central to her work. Hawthorne grew up in the charged atmospheres of Hong Kong and Northern Ireland - with a broad cultural mix as her constant visual tutor. This resource has helped to make her the

foremost interpeter of London's young jazz scene: the artist its artists want for their portraits, album sleeves and reportage.

"My work is about moments and people," says Hawthorne. "I've always loved drawing in the middle of any atmosphere: pubs, restaurants, weddings, gigs. But I'm glad fate ended me up in London when it did. Because English culture is changing, the actual culture is warming up. It's developing a street life and a new music - the means to actually celebrate life. All the young artists I respect have been a part of cultural changes over the past few years. And you can see in their work a different kind of society starting to happen."

A desire for true creative community was part of the old punk legacy. "I'd like Rocking Russian to be the name for more than a graphic style," Al McDowell had said wistfully in 1980. "More to do with the kind of situation we've set up. We don't even give out the names of our designers - and we have a PR photo that's deliberately all in shadow. The name is a symbol of unity for us to hide behind."

Designers like Soul II Soul's Nicolai Bean (above, with her work in the initial Soul II Soul shop) and Derek Yates (who drew the strip below) learned from art-school and training courses. But they also studied popular art, in the form of record sleeves and comic-books. It helped them capture a special moment in London social history

Beat-Box Business Sense

The late-'80s underground scene - as participants quickly realised - was able to unite work and play. In this, it succeeded where previous social provocateurs (like Malcolm McClaren, who mounted a high-profile campaign for "piracy" at the inception of the '80s) had failed. And it empowered a new generation, many of them "minorities" or traditionally disenfranchised groups. Pirate skills did not require art school, technical college or any form of State education; they were learned directly from other people.

The '80s radio stations which typified this generation's aesthetic were not like their '60s forebears. Land-based, they broadcast from tower blocks and warehouses, rather than from ships at sea. And they survived by hustling; selling ads and hawking products (records, club nights, events) created by their own employees. Pay-for-play was often common practice. But illegal broadcasting sparked more widespread money-spinners: practices like bootlegging - the pressing and distribution of illicitly generated discs. Many such "booties" were original compositions, and those who had made them often went on to produce mainstream hits.

DJs, bootleggers, guerilla delivery-men, the sales staff in specialist stores - by the middle of the decade, these roles had become interchangeable. The Britons who ran clubs and shops also promoted them over the pirate airwaves. And the DJ who mixed a record might hand you the change when you bought it.

As more and more youngsters caught on, bootlegging spread to other fields: kids learned to make money selling copies of sportswear, T-shirts, designer clothes. Any logo was fair game - and once they had shifted a set of such goods, entrepreneurs might use the earnings to bankroll designs of their own. From bootlegging came a range of young businesses boasting colourful titles: Hardwire Videographics, Ahead of Our Time Music, Blueback Records, Insane Ironic Skate Clothing, Goodfoot Promotions, Poizone Designs.

The pirate entrepreneurs had shown that art could also mean business. Consequently, young Britons launched fanzines as "proper" publications little slicks with titles like Fresh Air or Soul Underground. They clubbed together to open shops, like West London's Culture Trend and Glasgow's Clan Skates. And, of course, they continued to stage regular clubs and one-off events. Kids were starting to realise they could control their work opportunities, design their own experience.

Above: the logo to Ged Wells' Insane clothing company

**1, THE MUSIC MAKER
2, THAT GREEDY BEAT
MATT BLACK
+
THE COLDCUT CREW**

As bootlegging boomed, new enterprises sprang up. Some were promotion companies (top), others cut new sounds (below, one of the Coldcuit partnership's stamps)

Pirate radio stations promoted improvisation, and the bootlegging they inspired spread from vinyl to clothing

Above left: a club flyer by Ian Swift mocks the idea of copyright with the Chanel logo; below left: Fila's sportswear logo meets the same fate; above right: St Martin's graduate Melanie Stevens got Rizla to sponsor her degree show, which she titled Skin Tight Tour '90

49

Inspiration to do so was not restricted to contact on the dancefloor or the encouragement of illicit airwaves. By the spring of '88, London's new leisure culture had generated a cache of new, specialist record shops right in the city centre. These outlets exist in a separate, if parallel, universe to giants like HMV, Tower and Virgin. Several - like Beak St's Red Records and D'Arblay St's Black Market - began life co-owned by black DJs; Soul II Soul shops are operated by the Soul II Soul collective.

These are proud new proprietors. And they knew that the way to build up trade is to use the personal touch. "You've got to make the kids feel important," says Steve Jerviere, of Black Market. "Just look at the person and take it from there."

The new shops became drop-in community centres, sites whose common denominator - music - brought together separate races and social groups in comfort. Lined with posters, festooned with T-shirts, counters covered with ticket stacks, they are the place to trade information and gossip, sounds, projects and style. In addition, with their overflowing bins, the stores serve as walk-in galleries of constantly changing dancefloor art.

"Black Market," noted Steve Jerviere in the autumn of '89, "is turning into a whole community. A place where people hang out, people talk to people, people get work and make deals with each other. We need spots like that, where kids can hang out and be influenced for the good."

Not everyone, of course, was pleased with the freelance hijacking of their insignia

Above: record shops like North London's Music Power provided semi-official postal addresses for pirate stations

Above: bootlegging soon meant the copying and appropriation of established, fashionable logos

DJ Steve Jerviere, co-founder of Soho's Black Market Records, in September of 1989: "It's all based in London now, the control and real inventiveness. It's 'cause we really take pride in our sounds. My Dad's into music, my older brother's got a great collection. We've got a groove, a nice, get-down groove America could never have. And it comes from where and how we grew up. You're not in the world for gain alone. You're in it to build something up."

The legalisation of London's KISS-FM on September 1, 1990 was a milestone of Dancefloor Justice, and a measure of the real influence the dancefloor style enjoyed. The three-year-old pirate station lost on its first application for a licence. But when it then won a frequency, Londoners were amazed by the panache which advertised its debut. They shouldn't have been: the duo behind the launch design, 26-year-old Tom Carty and 30-year-old Walter Campbell of BBDO were both clubbers and KISS-FM listeners. With six days to pitch for the station's account, they managed to translate years of flyers, fashion and good times into a smart, witty, urbane campaign. Part of its success was its deliberate use of dancefloor celebrities – like dancer Wumni Olaiya. Wumni had appeared as the silhouette inside Soul II Soul's debut LP (right). A fashion stylist (Caron Wheeler is one client), Olaiya also designs clothes for her own label, Revolution With Love. "Wumni has so many talents," says Carty. "She typifies that scene. And we knew her; we once gave her a lift home from a big party for Prince." The decisions Campbell and Carty took won KISS upscale attention. But it also showed "straight" London what the dancefloor was about: the comradeship and imagination; the great music and genuine style

In three years of pirate broadcasting, KISS-FM created image and a loyal following; it was a party young Londoners clearly wanted to attend. When the station went legal, the trick was to bring that "vibe" a visual appeal

PAUL ANDERSON   STEVE JERVIER

BOB JONES

JUDGE JULES

JAZZIE B   MAX IX &
DAVE VJ

MATT BLACK   GORDON MAC

DADDY BUG   JONATHON
MORE

COLIN DALE   NICK POWER

PETER   DENNI
DAVIS   RAMPLING

THE AU REVOIR PARTY
at the WAG

35 Wardour St., W1
Wednesday, 28th December '88
£6.00   First Come First Served
9.30pm – 3.30am

LEAVE YOUR REINDEER OUTSIDE

TONY FARSIDES   RICHIE RICH

COLIN FAVER   DEAN SAVONNE

PATRICK FORGE   JAY STRONGMAN

NORMAN JAY

HEDDI   H   DJ TEE

MADHATTER TREVOR

STEVE JACKSON   THE ZOO EXPERIENCE

LINDSAY WESKER

Kiss fm's *written* **WORD**

NO
LICENCE FOR
KISS FM
FULL DETAILS INSIDE

IMPROVE
YOUR
DANCING
WITH
A KISS.

house

garage

car

rap

kitchen

funk

jazz

junction

dance

street

soul

factory

kiss

THE STATION ON EVERYONE'S LIPS

Opposite page, Middle: "Au Revoir" party invite: Dec 28, 1988. Above: Wumni Olaiya in a BBDO KISS-FM launch poster. Near right: ticket to the station's first legal rave. Centre: ad in the Evening Standard newspaper. Far right: on launch day, even an ex-pirate attracted VIPs

Last Thursday of Every Month

TON-UP CLUB
THURSDAY 27th SEPTEMBER 1990
LIVE!

...TS
...UL FAMILY SENSATION
JOMANDA

DJs
STEVE JERVIER
DAVE PEARCE
MANASSEH
JUDGE JULES
PAUL 'TROUBLE' ANDERSON

ACADEMY
TICKETS £8 THE ACADEMY BOX OFFICE
211 STOCKWELL ROAD, LONDON SW9
TEL:071-326 1022

TOMORROW

Kiss
100 fm

ITALIANS CROSS
INTO JORDAN
(See Page One)
Thirteen Italian women and six

Printed & published by Evening Standard Co. Ltd, Northcliffe H

KISS 100 FM LAUNCH
SATURDAY, 1ST SEPTEMBER, 1990
DINGWALLS
CAMDEN LOCK, NW1
LAUNCH TIME 12 NOON

"We really wanted the KISS campaign," says BBDO's Tom Carty. **"It wasn't just some project, like Pepsi or chewing gum."**

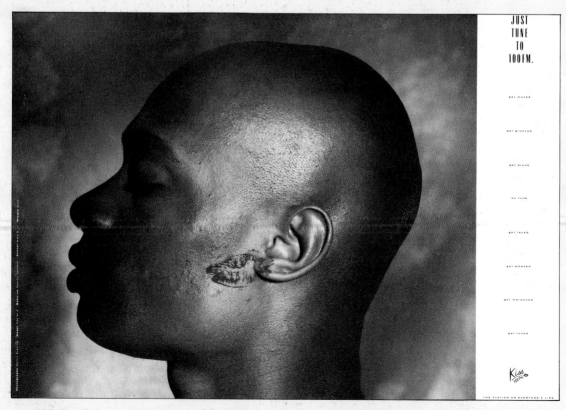

"All the ads", says Campbell, **"were similar in concept. We kept them in black and white, to make it stylish and crisp but to retain a street credibility."**

JOIN THEM ON 100FM.

THE STATION ON EVERYONE'S LIPS

Photography Roger Charity at Susi Purdy   **Production** Clare Blakemore   **Models** Barry Kamen at Storm   Tess at Unique   Tony Felix at Select   Renee Hodak at Premier   Vanessa King   Charles Pollington   Tamzin Greenhill at Models One   **Stylist** Mitzi   **Make-up** Kay   **Hair** Joseph Carney at Daniel Galvin

Left: one of BBDO's most popular posters was this one, which featured the original Buffalo boy, Barry Kamen, as a model. But KISS was a project everyone wanted to succeed; photographers, models and stylists worked on the campaign for credits, which then appeared on the ads. Many rapidly disappeared from their subway or bus-shelter sites

Comrades In Anarchy: Skateboarding Style

From clothing labels (above: Jamie Blair and Davey Phillips' Poizone) to carrier bags (below: by Savage Pencil), British skating has ebullient dancefloor style

By 1985, skateboarding had become the ultimate underground sport. But when it emerged above ground, its style and design talents dazzled

In fact, there are more such places: shops devoted to skateboarding. Like punk music, skateboard-riding or "skating" had become a full-blown craze in both the UK and US around 1976. But it dates from the California '60s, when it was seen as a sideline to ocean surfing.

The year of Britain's first great skate boom was 1977; by 1978, there were TV reports, UK skate parks, an English Skateboard Association.

Skater-artist Ged Wells in one of his own designs

But by 1979 it was seen as a thing of the past, a victim of the preteen BMX biking fad. In fact, skating merely went underground - to become another Situationist art. Its skills relied on the least comfortable, least "human" bits of the urban landscape: concrete and steel. And the underground culture they generated reflects the radical nature of that fact.

The sport's stars are young athletes with transglobal reputations: skaters paid to endorse the boards they ride and the clothes they wear. With whole companies built on their images and personalities, American stars like Powell-Peralta's "Bones Brigade" earn double- and triple-figure salaries.

They feature in global, glossy mags like America's Thrasher and Transworld Skateboarding.

By the mid-'80s, such skaters commanded the status of pop stars. They inspired videos, graphics, T-shirts and sportswear of their own. And, just as US teams began to recruit British skaters, UK companies (like Death Box) set out to garner a chunk of skate sales for themselves.

The word for skate artefacts - equipment, video, fashion and print - has to be gonzo. The psychology of the sport is individual and anarchic. Its graphic expressions are ultra-responsive to underground trends. And its real styles - like those of punk - are defined by D-I-Y. For the thing which made it a craze is skating's essential economy. All one needs to do it is the board, the terrain and the talent.

Music beats close to the heart of this beast - in the '80s, kids bearing skateboards became a frequent sight at gigs. And skating has created a language of its own. Since the 1970s, its underground has solidified into a whole culture. It has fearsome "skate gangs", revered skate designers (like Powell-Peralta's Craig Stecyk, Transworld's Grant Brittain and

Skateboarding requires little more than wheels and zeal. Yet it provides many and varied zones for design. Far left: wheels; centre: British skater Wurzel in 1988; right: skateboarding decks, which are customised by graphics

Initially Art Editor of RAD (Read and Destroy) magazine, skater-designer Nick Phillips turned his Anarchic Adjustment label (started in 1986) into a multi-national success. Today, at age 22, he exports to the UK, Japan and Europe from a new base in California. Says Phillips: "The creative energy and networking are both going crazy in England. But the really massive market for our stuff remains America." Below: the label of Phillips' 1990 collection

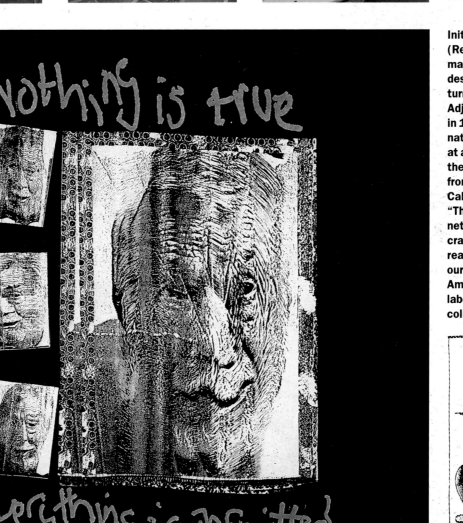

Thrasher's Gothic "Pushead" - aka Brian Shroeder), and favoured fashion accessories, like tattoos, earrings and dreadlocks.

Skating sites and competitions are spread across the world, so this culture used alternative media means to create a grapevine. At first, its chief organs were American magazines, fanzines and videos which helped convey the skills and excitement of top-class skating. By 1986, they had been almost supplanted by a one-on-one variant: the shops, like London's Slam City Skates, where such mags, boards and videos were sold. Slam City Skates shares a shop with Rough Trade Records, a specialist vinyl retailer founded during the heyday of punk.

Slam City's founder, Paul Sunman, says ties between skate culture and underground music have always been strong. "It makes perfect sense to share our site with a record shop," he said in 1988. "For two such diverse things to be so closely associated has been unusual in England. But it's getting more common every day." Sunman was right: three years later, London has 15 skate shops, including another branch of Slam City Skates (and Rough Trade Records) sited in Covent Garden. The London shops generate £12 million per annum from over 25,000 skaters - Britain's slice of 20 million skaters around the world.

Both Britons and visiting skaters help make stores like Slam City Skates and Carnaby St's M-Zone hangouts equivalent to the vinyl soul shops. And, just like those retail centres, skate shops serve as galleries for a variety of design. Their walls are lined with wooden "decks", selling on the strength of flamboyant graphics. Their racks bulge with skate clothes and their shelves are stacked with trainers - many of each destined to withstand dancefloor, rather than skate-park, use. Over the hot summers of '88 and '89, skatewear and skate aesthetics became essential costume at British raves.

In fact, skate-pop alliances permeated the 1980s. Bands as venerable as Psychic TV or as new as Jesus Jones used skate fashions to build their image. TV used the phenomenon to fill its "youth culture" slots. And suddenly British skaters (like Soul II Soul's Tony "Dobie" Campbell) were producing records, writing and designing books (Skateboarding Is Not a Book by Vernon Adams and Gavin Hills; The Skateboard Workbook by Steve Kane), and initiating fanzines, lines of clothing, nightclubs like Witchworld and South London's Method Air (which featured skateboard ramps). They did it all in style - with bright and electric colours which throbbed to a fast and active pulse.

British skaters demonstrate a strong bond to street aesthetics - whether this means graffiti by West London Pressure (a crew which includes skater Ricky Plant), clothing by skater Nick Phillips, or Insane Ironic sweatshirts designed by skater/artist Ged Wells. And in 1990, as British pop style colonised the United States, California skate videos changed course, to co-opt that style. Formerly slick, hyper-commercial artefacts, they suddenly took on the character of Britain's scrappy but highly individual skate scene. Titles for import videos priced at £25.95 (like World Enterprises' "Rubbish Heap"or the Foundation's "Glam Boys on Wheels: Too Cool to Skate") became downbeat and wry. And the films themselves aimed for a dirty, rebellious amateur vibe.

Mr Questionable Shoeman.

This page and opposite: Ged Wells began Jim-Jams to help support his mother, who screen-printed his designs at home in the Isle of Wight. By 1990, it had become a different company, Insane Ironic Skatewear

Hip Pouch

A nightclub artefact par excellence was the hip pack, first brought back from Japan by skater Dobie Campbell. Soon, they were designed by everyone from Ged Wells (left) to Michele Barnarse

nice Doggy!

Insane is the sort of company which showcased its 1990 collection at the Wag Club, in a rave where clothes were modelled by breakdancers

insane

Mouse is Pulling the Key

· Edwards Vacuumous Secret ·

In the Cupboard
Under the Stairs
Domesticated and
threatened by Science
appliance
Edward Hoover Spent many
years with silent friends
Friends in the dark, they
hated the dark.
            Edwards crime
Edward could reach the
light switch. Edward
lived in lazy cheating fear
If they should know, they
would hate Edward.
Edward in the cupboard
with friends in the dark.

A Bathelphant Moans
and Roams
the land
In Search
of a Shower attachment
'Vengeance Will be mine'

Like most British skaters, Wells is involved in several things. With Mouse Is Pulling the Key (left, centre), he made a skate video. Other work includes cartoons and children's books

RAD magazine required special art direction, which knew the performance of skateboarding "tricks". Its first Art Editor was Nick Phillips (layouts, top row), so punkish he tried to make the printers scan sandpaper-like grip tape from an actual deck. He was succeeded by book design vet Ian Lawson (layouts, second and third rows), who streamlined the magazine. In late 1990, Lawson left, and was replaced by ex-English Skateboarding Association President Dan Adams

Left: Zine by Brighton's Skate Muties; centre: Paul Browne's Sketchy; right: a club where punters skated

Opposite page: RAD magazine was the glossy version of skateboarding's many fanzines. By 1991, it was so successful that publisher Robert Maxwell purchased it. Below: Penguin's Fantail imprint commissioned Skateboarding Is Not A Book from skater-journalists Gavin Hills and Vernon Adams. Right: a Slam City logo by design team Battle of the Eyes (Chris Long and Edwin "Savage Pencil" Pouncey)

© 1987 BATTLE OF THE EYES FOR
SLAM CITY SKATES

SLAM CITY SKATES

Right: London's Slam City Skates commissoned its shop logo from Chris Long

Below, centre: Paul Sunman, the skater-photographer who founded London's Slam City Skates retail operation. Flanking him: the new import videos which have picked up on British skate style

"Everyone's trying to make them," said Paul Sunman who, through Slam City, sponsored Briton Ged Well's Mouse Is Pulling the Key vid. "And, thanks to super VHS and Hi8 video formats, almost anyone can. As a throwaway item, these videos have a casual, very fast turnover. And that's beginning to be reflected in their style." American corporations weren't the only ones interested in the lively aesthetics of Britain's skateboarding scene. Some of the UK's quirkiest young designers also found it irresistible. Illustrators such as Ian Wright and Chris Long leapt at the chance to design new "decks". And cartoonist Savage Pencil (aka Edwin Pouncey) executes Slam City logos, stickers and sweatshirts as well as boards themselves.

Eighties skate culture intersected with the dancefloor explosion because both share an interest in self-expression, style, film, and pop culture - in addition, of course, to music. Each admits no boundaries between art and life, between work and enjoyment. And the cultures share slang and guerilla communication (fanzines, posters, "tickets") the way they share fashion and sounds.

But when it comes to graphic translation, UK skating's native anarchy has been tamed by British classicism. Skateboarding Is Not a Book, designed by Penguin's Dave Crook, attempts (with stretched and squashed type, twisted and distorted colour) to catch the heady mix of the culture. But it also tries to render those orbits accessible to any consumer.

At RAD (for "Read And Destroy") magazine, the same principle applies. Born from a BMX bike mag which folded in 1986, the 60,000-reader glossy is now Britain's foremost skate magazine. From summer 1988 through 1990, skater Ian Lawson served as its Art Director. "A designer who didn't understand skating would be lost," says Lawson. "Because you've got to know what makes a picture special: the move, the person involved, the site. There's a lot of design associated with skating - ads, clothing, shoes, decks. But most of that is product design, done by illustrators. It's not like putting together a skateboarding magazine."

To evolve a RAD identity, Lawson looked to Britain and Europe rather than to those American mags (Transworld and Thrasher) which have dominated the market. "They've been very influential. But they also try too hard. They'll put half a word on a page so you have to turn it to read the title. Or bury a title within the spread. You can't have design impact which shortchanges skating itself."

Lawson preferred design to embody the action and the comradeship which permeate skate culture. And this, says RAD founder Tim Leighton-Boyce, is the sort of designer he needs. "Ian trained at Kall-Kwik printers as well as Fontana paperbacks. And that's what we require. Skating doesn't need people who want to try and do a Brody: emphasise and draw attention to their contribution, their personality. That's not what it's about."

So sound system theory inspires the skate community much as it does the soul underground. After all, it is perfectly suited to serve student idealism - not to mention a teen's traditional craving to belong. And it can fuel the dreams of young Britons longing for a potential denied them within "official" UK society.

Above: Edwin "Savage Pencil" Pouncey's Skate Bug deck design. Below: skaters Jason Florio (left) and Gavin Hills (right) model home-made skate designs

Smiley Says: The Odyssey Of Acid House

Once launched, the Smiley face became an unstoppable symbol. Top: DJ Tim Simenon's global No 1 record, "Beat Dis"; below: In 1991, designer Tony Cooper re-interpreted the Smiley on a Boy George sleeve

The dancefloor brought together disparate youth groups: jazz snobs and football fans, educated kids and those whose parents drove subway trains

One example of such inspiration-by-sound is West London native Trevor Jackson. In 1987, he was a 19-year-old nightlife enthusiast with little to offer beyond ideas and boundless energy. "I went to West Barnet College," says Jackson, "then I applied to St Martin's and all the other London colleges. Every one turned me down."

But Martin Huxford of Kunst Art Company (who taught at West Barnet) took him on as a part-time assistant. After two months, Jackson decided to "go for it" on his own. And his one-man studio Bite It! was born - with bright yellow business cards and a corner of Kunst Art Company turf. Amid the small print in Record Mirror, Jackson searched for potential clients. Then he would try, in person, to charm the relevant powers-that-be. Before long, he had stocked a large portfolio of sleeve-art: visualisations of house music and hip-hop, done for small labels who needed to give their image a boost.

What first brought Jackson notice was the Afro-urban imagery he developed for New York

Acid changed the whole club scene

rap act the Jungle Brothers (licensed in the UK by Gee St Records) in late '88. These rude, totemic caricatures in sneakers and nouveau voodoo get-up sprang from the designer's love of comics and Hanna-Barbera cartoons. And the Afrocentric vibe they expressed was the upcoming fashion of London's nightlife.

"Initially," laughs Gee St supremo John Baker, "Trevor came in with a demo tape: some rap music of his own. Later, he read we had signed the Brothers. And then he came steaming back, saying, 'Look! I'm also a graphic designer!'" Jackson, says Baker, has "brilliant" ideas. "And he vibes well with all our people."

"I'm out clubbing at least twice a week," explains Jackson, now 22. "So I know what I'm talking about; that's something people appreciate when I come in to see them."

Jackson's elan and eclecticism are partly the consequence of the radical social mix brought to London by dancefloor culture. Under its pirate tutelage, the capital became a world of flamboyant contradictions. Skateboarders carried mobile phones. DJs led double lives, stacking and selling records by day; flying to Milan or Paris at weekends to spin the very same discs. Raves like those by Westworld were 6,000-strong, money-making festivities with lavish themes (for one an entire fairground was built inside Brixton Academy). Yet tickets to them could only be bought in oddball, single sites: a boutique in Soho, a launderette on the New Kings Rd.

The '80s dancefloor brought together previously discrete youth groups. Skateboarders and football freaks were exposed to "soul boys", indie fans to young jazz snobs; Oxbridge-educated kids met teens whose mothers and fathers worked on London Underground. The subcultures absorbed each other's styles - and co-opted bits and pieces from one another's worlds.

These quirks and paradoxes paralleled Britain's civic landscape in the '80s: a fusion of futurism and squalor, where Dickensian beggars brushed shoulders with yuppie swells. Into this London, in the late summer of '87, swirled the phenomenon which became known as Acid House. It came from the capital's most colourless southern suburbs: Croydon, Southwark, Bermondsey. But acid's real birthplace was Ibiza, off the coast of Spain.

There young working-class Londoners on cheap package vacations frolicked in clubs called Star, Pasha, Amnesia and Esparadise - all-night danceterias whose playlists married House music to Euro-beat and rock. There they shopped for new fashions (mainly Spanish or Italian designer clothes) in stores with names like Trip and Magic. And there they discovered, wholesale, the drugs which would go with it: old-fashioned acid and "designer drug" Ecstasy.

House music - urgent, urban disco from gay, black, suburban Chicago - was popular in Britain long before such holiday-makers came home. Having come from a gay scene, its ethic was always fantasy-based. All "Acid" really added was one simple, identifiable sound: the oscillating trill of a Roland TB 303 synthesizer. But the music which resulted sparked Britain's first mass youth movement since punk. Acid house would extend the social mix begun by London's "rare groove" right across the nation. And illicit raves would soon attract not five-figure attendance, but crowds which numbered double thousands.

From its inception, Acid house was quintessentially suburban. "It was holiday-makers and scruffy skateboarders," says 22-year-old Tony Farsides, who reported the phenomenon for pirate station KISS-FM. "Just smoking dope and dancing and getting out of it. South London boys wearing beads with designer clothes; dirty Van sneakers and headscarves; sweatshirts and psychedelic colours."

Acid quickly found its own club - DJ Danny Rampling's Shoom, in a

Boys' Own, the fanzine which broke acid from cult status to way of life

South London fitness centre. Then it produced Boys' Own, the self-published, 60p fanzine which broke the cult. Boys' Own founders Terry Farley and Paul Oakenfold (both, of course, DJs) were quick to lead their soccer-loving nouveau-hippie flock to the head of London's Next Big Thing. Shoom moved uptown, into the capital's clubland central. And UK fashion freaks took up "acid" - as did the music papers, the drug-sniffing gutter press and youthful shoppers on every high street.

As soon as house music mutated into Acid house, records were re-titled to capitalize on drug references - and the market was flooded with "microdot mixes" or "sunshine dubs". And designers of sleeve art, promotional posters, fashion spreads, flyers - even street graffiti - aimed for a visual equivalent. They were helped by the movement's unofficial logo: the so-called "Smiley face" familiar from beneficent '60s hippiedom.

The Smiley - flyer-symbol of Shoom, thanks to designer George Georgiou, who had landscaped RAW in '86 - had been picked up off the cover of cult comic The Watchmen. Created in 1986 by writer Alan Moore and artist Dave Gibbons, the dynamic rhythms, constant in-jokes and shifts of time and place this "graphic novel" contained made it a visual parallel to the aural arts of mixing and sampling. An update of comic-books, graphic novels like The Watchmen provided another facet of late-'80s guerilla communications. D-I-Y publishing had advanced

Sign of the times
Present clobber from
Duffers
Stussy
Custard Shop
Dominic de Bruxelles
Sign of the times
Jimmy Jumble
Boys Own
Kangol
S.Tek
Jewellery
Billy Boy
& a range of
one-off clobber.
1st floor Kensington Mkt
Kensington High St. 071 376 0762

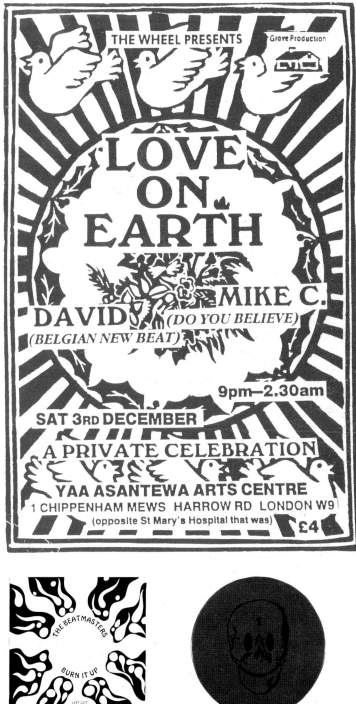

THE WHEEL PRESENTS Grove Production

LOVE ON EARTH

DAVID MIKE C.
(BELGIAN NEW BEAT) (DO YOU BELIEVE)

9pm—2.30am

SAT 3RD DECEMBER

A PRIVATE CELEBRATION

YAA ASANTEWA ARTS CENTRE
1 CHIPPENHAM MEWS HARROW RD LONDON W9
(opposite St Mary's Hospital that was) £4

THE BEATMASTERS
BURN IT UP

As the acid fad grew to huge proportions, it altered flyer art, scrambling styles (top left) and leading handouts towards the dreamy old hippy world familiar from the day of illustrator Roger Dean (top right). Below left: microdot mix from The Beatmasters; below right: even Psychic TV went for the Smiley face

A wave of finer feelings hit clubland after Prince played Wembley Arena in Summer '88. Even jewellery designers like Richard Dyer (below left) were affected

Born in a South London fitness centre, Danny and Jenny Rampling's Shoom Club became the premier acid venue, when it took the West End by storm

substantially from the smudgy samizdat era of punk, and comic art was a prime beneficiary. Like football fanzines (On the Ball, When Saturday Comes, Footie), skateboard mags (RAD; Skateboard!, Skate Action), and graffiti-artist publications (Freestyle, Positronic, Homeboy), comics like Deadline and Crisis encroached on the turf of the young style press. The first comic-book to formalise such an objective and survive was Escape - a fanzine begun in '82 by Paul Gravett and Peter Stanbury.

Escape was the first such 'zine to gain WH Smith distribution. But during the 1980s, the need for "proper" distribution would disappear. Publications would be sold directly at raves or through the alternative retailers: record and skate-shops, fashionable boutiques. "The fanzine now has more power than the established lifestyle mags," marvelled Titan Books' publicist Don Melia in late '88. "There's a real youth network operating now. Just take one image, the acid Smiley face. DJ Tim Simenon's Bomb the Bass took that from Dave Gibbons. Now, it's everywhere. Every trader in the High Street is trying to sell it back to the kids. The High Street is watching what the mainstream media try to ignore!"

By 1988, there were Acid scarves, Acid remix chart hits, Acid newspaper columns and daily scandal stories about the cult. The slightly monotonous music (and its attendant dancefloor war-cry, "ACCCIIIEEED!!") wiped almost everything else off the British playlist. London record companies had always liked house music - because the

tracks were cheap to buy. This time, the industry itself was prepared to accept a street fad, and Acid grew to giant proportions.

"The Acid scene converted thousands and thousands of people," said Black Market's Steve Jerviere in September '89. "People who were probably never interested in music before - all they knew about it was Duran Duran or the next teenybop thing on telly. Now, because of all the exposure, everybody's into the look, the records, the whole package."

Richard Satnarine, the 24-year-old manager of G&M ("Groove & Move") Records, London's largest wholesaler of dancefloor vinyl, put it another way. "Without Acid house, our sales would have died in the summer of '87. Maybe it was only a fad - but it saved my industry's ass."

The deep feeling which powered "rare grooves" and the comradeship of Acid house raves also sparked something more profound: a rediscovery of spiritual drives. Youngsters who turned to Britain's official art scene for self-expression found only social inertia and formal exhaustion - the opposite of that warmth and excitement generated by the dancefloor. They also perceived the establishment's ruling Eurocentricity, its absence of any interest in other cultures and foreign worlds.

Package trips abroad had already put young Britons in touch with the populist expression of other countries' votive arts: charms, shrines, sacred icons. So had exhibitions like the Hayward Gallery's Diego Rivera show and the Serpentine Gallery's The Life of the Dead in Mexican Folk

Above: religious souvenirs from package holidays abroad influenced the nascent psychedelia of acid-era design and publishings. Below: sleeve art began to investigate typefaces through other religions (here, Tony Cooper for MC Kinky)

Art, both in 1987. The cultural democracy embodied in such work piqued developing British desires; it fed the longing for a sacred imagery which could be applied to individual lives.

Then, in midsummer '88, pop singer Prince brought his lavish "Lovesexy" tour to Wembley Arena. The Afro-American funk religion which fuelled his two-hour shows was heady stuff - showcasing the sexual impulse as a key to transcendence, the ephemeral groove as a clear signifier of the eternal. At the heart of a show which included onstage Cadillacs, bed romps and man-size mechanical flowers was the solitary moment when Prince, unaccompanied, had the audience join him in singing his hymn "The Cross".

The massive clout of these Wembley shows - not to mention their consummate theatricality - was all the underground needed. By autumn, dancefloors were swamped with explicitly religious ciphers. Those ecstatic gospel roots which had nourished soul and funk fused with the Acid-induced exaltation of the raves. And the response included badges that featured Jesus and the Pope; T-shirts emblazoned with Day-Glo Madonnas; clubs with names like Love, Ascension, Trance, High On Hope, The Last Temptation, Spirit of Ecstasy. In Kensington Market, the Marx & Stalin boutique of mid-'80s fame re-christened itself "Big Jesus Trashcan", and took to importing religious knick-knacks from the Continent. The spiritual search of Acid had begotten hardcore, dancefloor business.

Graphic Confrontation: The Guerilla Copy Shop

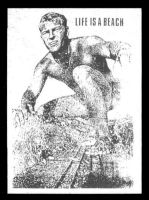

LIFE IS A BEACH

Above: a page from Mark Jackson's Positronic echoes the slogan of a popular skatewear label; below: graffiti influenced this club ticket by Jackson

London's dancefloor culture forged changes that mattered; it altered the marketplace of pop and the impulse behind young design

In the early days of '60s pop art, pundits as well as the public found it hard to differentiate the new art objects from their sources. ("Even now, I suspect," wrote critic Ellen Johnson in 1976, "to the uninitiated, Oldenburg's sculptures are still food and clothing . . . Lichtenstein's paintings are comics . . . and Warhol's are news photographs.") During the 1980s, British social critics found it hard to admit that the changes forged by London's dancefloor mattered. Media brokers whose relationship with the US has hinged for years on images like those of Alistair Cooke introducing TV's Masterpiece Theatre have difficulty accepting Soul II Soul as an influential artistic export.

Portrait of Stravinsky by Ian Wright

Nevertheless, the onetime outlaw culture profoundly changed both the marketplace of pop and the impulse behind young British design. It altered the actual configuration of young UK society. Led by a black aesthetic which rallies to the transcultural cry "Express Yourself", dancefloor movers and shakers taught their punters that art, work and fulfilment in life need not be separate pursuits. That belief was the most creative act. That money, position - even resources - matter less than good ideas, ingenuity and perseverance. Club culture demonstrated less-than-orthodox ways in which community could be constructed: out of basic differences, as well as from similarities.

In these respects, the style-conscious world of the dancefloor reprised the most romantic tenet of British punk experience: the conviction that absolutely anyone can do it. This Do-It-Yourself ethic pervaded late-70s music and design - and many post-punk activists and shakers carried it with them into the decade of mix records, digital sampling and flyer art. The new scene attracted those who once had hoped for more than punk could deliver: designers like Terry Jones, artists like Ian Wright. And their involvement spiked pirate activism with expertise from an older and more experienced group.

The Copyart collective in 1986, photographed for the London Daily News by Dick Scott Stewart, shortly before they re-located from their original premises to a larger site in London's Kings Cross area. Below: their moving card

Painter-designer Ian Wright made his name putting face to sound each week in New Musical Express; his expressionistic portraits accompanied fresh album reviews. Wright retains strong connections with music - and he welcomed the revolution of Britain's late-'80s. "Graphics changed completely after the punk and the Brody eras," says Wright. "Because it established a bit of a different design formula, punk gave lots of people a way in. But, working for themselves, they just became the next establishment. . . . It doesn't help that in England designers are seen as doing one thing and one thing only. If you're good at drawing rabbits people never think you might like to try and draw a horse. The new generation is kids who refuse to just keep pumping out rabbits!"

Wright became involved with young designers through two studios where he worked: the Unknown, from 1985 to 1989, and the Neville Brody Studio, where he shares space today. Some of the kids who sought him out for collaborations, he says, were the same who, in earlier days, "used to clip my work out of NME."

Like them, Wright loves house, hip-hop, ragamuffin rap. And he prizes the textures and thieveries made possible by sampling. "For visual types, it's so inspirational. 'Cause that message is: Use the technology. Graphics is not an old man's medium anymore; the day when you sit down and draw a car is gone forever."

The Apple Mac, Quantel Paintbox, and Scitex computers are perfect for such designers, who want to push parameters. But, below a certain budget, the tool of choice and change remains the humble colour copier; used as often for i-D's graphics as for throwaway tickets to clubs.

And artists like Mark Jackson, a 28-year-old refugee from advertising art, prefer the punk tool of xerox collage to any brand of computer. Jackson's work has appeared in Vogue and been cited by Creative Review. But rather than cast his lot in with an agency or design firm, he spent six months apprenticed to 24-year-old Londoner Ricky Plant. Plant coached him in graffiti: the ultimate strechno art.

71

Left: a piece from Laurie Rae Chamberlain's first exhibit, State of Vector, held at the Acme Gallery in 1976. It featured xeroxes of his address book and led to a subsequent show at London's Institute of Contemporary Art

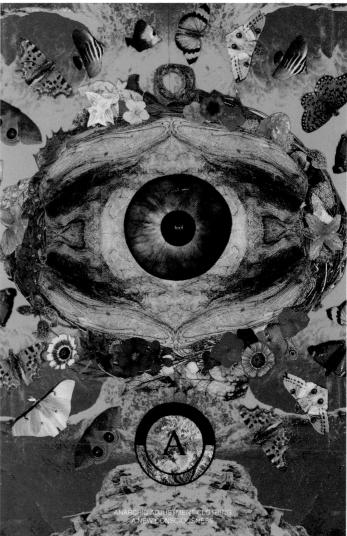

Above left: xerox art by Mark Jackson; right: an ad for Nick Phillips' Anarchic Adjustment which utilises acid-era Mind Power motifs via photocopier funkiness. Xerography has become an accepted facet of "street-conscious" illustration and visual art

Below left: "Salvador" from Laurie Rae Chamberlain's 1980 Post-Modern Cards exhibition. Right: xerox-inspired portrait of rappers Run DMC, who wrote "My Adidas", by Ian Wright. Wright, who strives to incorporate extra texture and dimension into his work, spraypainted shoelaces as a background

"Strechno" is Jackson's personal term for the arts of guerilla communication: the "bombing and "tagging" of street graffiti; the owner-proprietor orbits of desktop publishing; the funky universe of xerography and "scratch xerox". As a fringe art form, xerography can be traced back to another independent spirit: Laurie Rae Chamberlain, one of the first post-Jamie Reid designers to link colour xerox and sound. Chamberlain's first exhibit (in 1976) reproduced his address book; his second featured xeroxes of how the book had changed. For both, he employed the first colour xerox machine in Britain. "It was at one end of Heathrow Airport, under where Concorde takes off. I kept thinking about that, because one of my favourite records then was 'Oooo There Goes Concorde Again', by the Native Hipsters."

Xerox colour copiers are over twenty years old, yet they have never ceased to provide the perfect "modern" aura. "The light which passes under the image," explained Chamberlain in 1980, "is a neon light. The colours xerox artists cultivate are hot, vibrant colours. And the process is an instant one. All that seems very modern. But, really, the links with music date all the way back to Andy Warhol - to how he did his silk-screen process and the images he chose."

When the Institute of Contemporary Art gave Chamberlain an exhibition in July of 1978, he called it STP(X), for "Six Talented People Xeroxed". It contained huge, collaged xerox portraits - punk personality Jordan, stylist Susie Slack - complete with collaged "gold frames" around their edges. STP(X) was a huge success, attracting massive fan mail and the approbation of artists such as Allen Jones and Peter Blake. And Chamberlain continued his xerographic comment on celebrity in the early '80s. But more and more of his work was commissioned from Japan. And the rest was mostly to publicise fringe music ensembles - bands like the Flying Lizards and Canned Heat; Crass, Stiff Little Fingers, Prince Far I.

In 1985, the Greater London Council recognised the colour copier as the struggling designer's favourite tool. They funded a "Photocopying Resource Centre" and called it Copyart. Copyart, which has survived its founder, offers budget-rate access to paper, copiers, computers - even an "image bank". Over the five years of its existence, its workshops in schools and community centres have made self expression as well as smalltime publishing accessible to a broad range of Britons.

The collective which administrates these resources continues to prove that xerox art need not be small, cheap, dull or didactic. (Some of their complex, quilt-size hangings suggest updates of Victorian and Edwardian union banners.) And, in the late '80s and early '90s, Copyart has broadened its scope to include the promotion of outside exhibits: xerography shows with titles like Artstrike, CopyArt, Life As We Know It.

It continues to serve the clients it was initially founded to help: agitprop groups, women's organisations, community associations. But it is used more and more by outriders from the new leisure world: guerilla design and art operatives. They need its assets for flyers, posters, and sleeve-art. Or, in a case like Allan Parker's, for something even more eclectic.

Parker is a qualified arts therapist and martial arts practitioner who,

Supplied by Vibes Records and Tapes, 3 Princess Parade, Bury, Lancs
Tel: 061 764 3013

Pic by Kate Simon

PATTI SMITH: an Alternative Number 10.

I think it's crap! I think she's so awful . . she's full of rubbish, she's full of words and crap. I mean, she's a poseur of the worst kind, intellectual bullshit, trying to be a street girl when she doesn't seem to me to be one, I mean, everything . . . a useless guitar player, a bad singer, not attractive.
Mick Jagger 78

Laurie Rae Chamberlain 78

Andy Warhol and xerography pioneer Laurie Rae Chamberlain (left) shared a lot. Chamberlain's use of the copier echoed Warhol's screenprinting techniques, and both made underground films. Both also commented on the nature of fame; early Chamberlain works included studies of Elvis in his coffin and murderess Ruth Ellis as well as the likes of Adam Ant. (Above) Laurie Rae Chamberlain portrait of Patti Smith from his World's End exhibition

When pirate DJ Tim Westwood went legal on Capital Radio, he gave hip-hop fans and graffiti crews access to the commercial airwaves

since 1988, has taught video technique at the Polytechnic of Central London. In a separate capacity, he designs slide-show art. His work encapsulates the three-dimensional nature of nightlife as event, but also the sophistications of '80s image mixology. And Parker achieves these effects through the simplest D-I-Y processes of image manipulation: xerox, hand-tinting, the use of a TV screen.

His work is made to be shown at concerts and celebrations. And his initial impetus came from a housewarming in '85. "I had moved into this new flat with some old projectors sitting around. So I told everyone who came to bring along a slide. I had a wide-angle lens, so their projections filled one wall. I just left it on a dissolve and stuck in some collages I'd made."

One of Parker's guests was pop star Kim Wilde, who liked his own slides so much she commissioned a series for her next show. The enjoyment of finishing these gave Parker a brand-new idea: to make and publish a series of postcards. Then Parker met Wire's Paul Elliman - who commissioned a slide-show for the magazine's National Jazz Awards in 1987. The resulting series, Night-Town, occasioned a further commission from hi-fi retailers The Cornflake Shop.

Parker slide-shows have since been used for all kinds of social events - from music conferences to Sushi Evenings at the Cobden Men's Working Club; from concerts in Kuala Lumpur to nightclubs in Tokyo. All are set to music, and all operate very simply. "All you need," says Parker, "Is the slide machine and a tape-deck - two small black boxes."

But the simplicity is as deceptive as the mix on a Public Enemy twelve-inch. Parker: "Basically I xerox photos, then hand-tint, manipulate and size them up. Then I shoot each piece as a 35mm slide. I put the art work on the floor, point a video camera and plug it directly into a monitor - so the image comes up on a screen. Using the controls on the monitor, I fiddle and bring all the colours up."

This homogenises material which can range from hand-coloured xerox collage to computergraphics and specially staged photographs. "Anyone

could do it," says Parker. "But a lot of time is involved in finding things that will work together." When a series is projected, slides will be superimposed - adding depth and magic to the ethereal jumble of imagery. Atmosphere at every event also plays its part. Here, for instance, is Parker describing The Sushi Show in situ:

The whole thing came about through a chef called Simon Browne, who doesn't really like to do his cooking in restaurants. He specialises in staging meals that are more like rituals or happenings. And he started to do these "sushi nights" in a Working-Men's club in Ladbroke Grove, located next to some warehouses. The street was very dark and deserted, yet it would fill up with all these trendies - people like Jack Nicholson and Julien Temple.

The sushi was cooked onstage; that was made into a real production. And Simon had artists from Madame JoJos doing this risque floor-show in drag. Except for bits of the stage, the whole place was lit by candlelight. So it was very dark and we projected onto the walls. They were crumbly and distempered, so it looked like an ancient Italian church. The idea was to look like old frescoes, but with the images constantly changing.

For The Sushi Show, Parker used material found in bookshops - etchings he photocopied and manipulated - as well as three-dimensional objects he placed on black velvet to photograph. But soon he was originating imagery of his own. And in 1987, he met Andy Golding, who also taught at PCL. Golding was keen to help expand the slide projects into large-scale shows. So Parker and Golding struck a deal with their academic employer. "We use the show for teaching at PCL: to show what can be done with their equipment. That gives us access to their facilities."

The aim, says Parker, is to produce "a cross between a narrative and a mood piece. Something which gains its cohesiveness over a length of time. It's images which dissolve into, and add to, other images. A lot of it has to do with representing your imagination."

Fast-Frame For The Future

Coming up from the outside, Britain's new underground rulers of style are the bad boys of raggamuffin reggae. Above: the mark of early star Tiger; below, Shabba Ranks

From raggamuffin style to commercial video, record sleeves to T-shirts, young designers learned to respect each other's cultures and options

A new imagination, a poetry for their poetic moment, that's what the dancefloor designers seek. And they do not fight shy of emotion when discussing it. "I like an underground," says Trevor Jackson. "A real underground moment, when things become truly precious to you. I just want fun, yeah? Really strong concepts, good ideas and lots of excitement."

He says this is why he respects people like Soul II Soul and the Thunderjockeys. "Their stuff has that excitement and they're

Above: Clive Woodstock's ragga style

consummate businessmen. Yet you look at their work and it doesn't stink of money. Look at things by Peter Saville or Kasper de Graaf and you want to put a compass to their heads! It's so po-faced."

Unlike many design celebs who came out of the punk '70s, talents like Jackson seek something wider than personal fame. Creative Hands is a new studio founded in early 1990 by three black Britons - Paul Baptiste, Everton Wright and Donald Thomas. They run their design group the way others run nightclubs: at night and at weekends. Wright and Baptiste also maintain 9-to-5 jobs in other organisations: Wright at Soho's Design Solution, Baptiste at i-D magazine.

"What we see in the mainstream marketplace," says Wright, "is the way things become so big - both organisations and egos - that designers lose all the identity in their work. To support their egos and lifestyles, they start taking on anything they can get in the door. You see people leave design behind and get into what they buy: cars, clothes, computers. They forget the people! We come from a different place, a totally separate angle."

Creative Hands have occupied their premises - partly financed by East London's Hackney Council - only a short time. (The Council took more than a year to process the trio's Business Plan.) But the team has already handled work as diverse as fashion promotions, record sleeves, a set of

NEW SCOTLAND YARDIE

Below: Clive Woodstock's T-shirts for East London's Big, Broad and Massive

A long way from the sound systems (below) of old-line stars like Coxsone, ragga style aims for machismo and flash. Its persona draws on fashion but also on gangster sass

PUMP UP THE VOLUME

Far left: portrait of Bunny Wailer by Ian Wright; near, top: 12" record sleeve by Creative Hands; near, bottom: 7" record sleeve by Trevor Jackson/Bite It! Opposite page: logo by Trevor Jackson/Bite It!

fine-art poster designs inspired by Rigoletto and a corporate re-design for black housing association KUSH. Their aim, says Wright, is "to build a team of black talents that will make us one of this country's top design firms." It is sound system theory again - the use of individual skills to advance a collective aim.

Creative Hands was founded around a formal design-studio structure. But sound system theory can just as easily draw from politics. Artist Clive Woodstock caricatures pop-cultural idols - figures from boxer Nigel Benn to "ragamuffins", or reggae hustlers. Over the past three years, his T-shirts and posters have become familiar sights at clubs, concerts and London's annual Notting Hill Carnival. But Woodstock is not just a solitary talent; his work is promoted by part of Hackney Youth In Progress: "Big, Broad & Massive Promotions".

BBM is the "fund-raising arm" of this voluntary youth organisation (established in 1983 to protest the death in custody of young black Briton Colin Roach). "Instead of raising money through jumble sales and raffles," says a Youth In Progress spokesman, "we make and merchandise videos, art, music and live events."

The "Clive Woodstock Livestock Selection", a set of stickers, T-shirts and posters, is one of their strongest sellers. And its items are available both via mail order and through regular sites in London street markets. Woodstock's ongoing satire thus remains reactive - with outlets tailored to suit young consumers who are out and about. And, like all dancefloor design, the "vibe" it seeks to capture is a shared, collective affair.

Dancefloor designers see the challenge of teamwork - either constant or occasional - as more rewarding than individual celebrity. Even those who are not formally part of group arrangements exist as pieces of unofficial, floating aggregates: friends who consult or collaborate. "I think now," says Ian Swift, "instead of London designers competing, there's a great sense of mutual admiration. The people concerned are less insecure. And they don't care what the design press says, 'cause they never thought it would notice them."

The design tasks at hand, say his colleagues, are far more interesting. How do you visualise the change - social and perceptual - that '80's underground set in motion? When rap music altered what naming something means, how do you start to re-frame the naming functions of type? As the borders between different disciplines blur, how do you go about announcing it through design?

"We now want to work in a place where words and images flow together," says Thunderjockey Graham Elliott. "Where graphics begin and theatre ends. Use images as typography: mix image and typography so they flow into and from one another."

Jon Klein, producer of MTV's Buzz, was Head of Graphics for the music channel throughout the late '80s. During that time, he worked on several projects with the Thunderjockeys. "The great thing with them," he says, "is they're thrilled by every possibility: sound, colour, movement - the lot. They're childlike without being childish or faux-naif or calculated."

Klein touches on a fact at the heart of dancefloor design: all its practitioners dig the state of their art. Zealous as well as critical, they visualise what they feel - a delight in being alive that is all too rare in mainstream Britain. "The designer's job," says Trevor Jackson, "is to make the world look better. Things should be colourful, things should be bright. There's too little love of what they do in most people's work today." What such lively eyes seek to frame is a fresh British design. And they're proud to see their arts make a break with the established custodians of power. "In Britain there's still such a cult of tradition and respectability," notes Allan Parker. "With the Arts Council, with art directors, with agencies, with video. The same people are on the books again and again and again. But that system bears no connection to the quality of the work they deliver."

In place of this, the dancefloor evolved a language and business sense of its own. Depending on mutual respect, it functions by mutual support. And the young designers involved say that it can hold the blueprint for Britain's future. Thunderjockey John England: "There are loads of people out there with talent, a new British think-tank of personality. People who can - and will - make chairs and films and monsters as well as the covers for paperback books."

Ian Wright
Painter and Decorator

Ian Wright's vivid interpretations of sound with fury found their first wide expression in the weekly review pages of New Musical Express. There, his vision of a new LP would be scanned with as much curiosity as the reviewer's own verdict. As a consequence, musicians themselves soon jumped the gun to hire him first. Wright has designed and illustrated record sleeves for Pete Townshend, the Jam, King Sunny Ade, Cabaret Voltaire, Depeche Mode, the Last Poets, Black Uhuru, Run DMC, Factory Records, Island, Virgin and EMI.

But he never took the legendary NME slot as seriously as those art students who hoarded his illustrations. "I always thought of it as throwaway," he says. "It was just this fast blast of a job. Get the record on a Friday, listen and work over the weekend, hand in the piece Monday morning. When I went on to record sleeves, I was refining what I'd already heard and seen. What was good about NME was that readers already knew what the people I drew looked like. I could deal with the idea of the pop star."

Now, says Wright, "the influence has shifted. Sound systems, rappers and clubs carry the swing. Often the record company happens to be the last to know." He welcomes the changes, which he sees as returning the initiative to the designer. "It's harder to be honest about it and make a living, which matters to me 'cause I've got kids. But it's good to have the challenge of capturing something really new. Companies put 'music' in one little square and try to keep it there."

Wright has never seen it that way. "If you can visualise Mike Tyson or Public Enemy, you can draw Elmore Leonard - or Rudolf Nureyev." But 'drawing' is a misnomer when it comes to Ian Wright's technique. A reggae fan who favours Studio One artists, Harry Moodie, "Scratch" Perry and Burning Spear, Wright's stated ambition has been "to mash things up".

This parallels the cut-and-mix of hip-hop and the "versioning" of his West Indian idols. "Reggae is

Upper left: portrait of boxer Mike Tyson at the height of his fame, for American Esquire (acrylic); top: logo for Island Records' video series Rhythms of the World. Below: LP cover for "The Best of Jacob Miller" (gouache)

This page: a portrait of Sting for
Arena magazine uses one of
Wright's favourite techniques,
xerox and tissue paper

Wright used an early portrait series in New Musical Express as his laboratory for experiments in mixed media. An image of John Cooper Clarke (far left) is created from a rubber stamp of the punk poet's name. Sting (left) is "drawn" out of unwound used cassette tape. And this Rorschach image of the Psychedelic Furs (below right) is rendered in acrylic

brilliant. It teaches you to hear all these voices from different eras, different backgrounds. Some are actually dead, others are really young. The combination gives you something sophisticated, but very human - with quite a worldly texture."

Wright seeks such texture himself. He will crumple paper, stencil and xerox, spray and glue and layer. For a portrait of early rappers Run DMC, he laid actual shoelaces over his art work and gave the lot a graffiti spray. He painted musical visionary Sun Ra on a piece of old wood. "Even photography has started to discover those sorts of sensation," he says. "Becoming 'distressed' and so on. It pushes the image towards art, and typography becomes much less important. It took the street to accomplish that change."

And Wright still favours another street tool: the humble office copier. "The xerox is very important. Because you don't have to know about it to find out what it can do. It's getting their hands on technology that has made young designers able to drive what's happening. Kids know more about computers than adults are prepared to learn."

Initially, Wright aimed more towards the conventional; at art school his idols were commercial: London's NTA Studios, George Hardie, Malcolm Harrison, Bob Lawrie and airbrush ace Bush Hollyhead. Then, in 1980, Wright saw an ICA exhibit entitled "Art/Pop Japan". It featured the work of Katsu Yoshida - an artist who approached rock portraiture through a dazzling array of styles.

"I saw that," says Wright, "and realised I could take it anywhere. I could use abstraction, texture, multiple image: all the things I loved." A Karl Wirsun poster for Screamin' Jay Hawkins was also influential: "It started me opening up things and folding them out, like a Rorschach blot."

Wright executes album sleeves, murals (he customised one wall in DJ Dave "M/A/R/R/S" Dorrell's home), skateboard decks, postcards and T-shirts - as well as executive portraits for business magazines. But he subjects every job, however unorthodox, to the same careful process of scrutiny, analysis and time-consuming experimentation. "I always design for commercial use. Not to be hung on a wall. But I don't work in magazines and on record sleeves because

thousands of people see them - I'm not bothered how many people see anything I do."

When others his age are guarding commercial careers, why did he throw in his with a younger, dancefloor set? "Because those things changed life in London: rap, pirate radio, Acid house. You can't pretend it didn't happen. There's another generation now, kids who were raised on Neville Brody's stuff, my stuff, punk."

Wright finds them stimulating. And he credits younger designers with changing something else. "In the past few years, a whole chain of unadventurous people has grown up. Cautious editors and art directors who, in the end, make you cautious too. Art directors want an easy life, you know. They're not prepared to go and see what's happening in the street. They want an agent they can ring up, a buffer between you and them.

"It's all about ideas," says Wright. "The idea of someone's music, the idea of who they are, is what you're working with. Or the idea of Mexico, the idea of Japan. There are some advantages in Britain's being an island; the ambience of a dancefloor is about that sort of ideas."

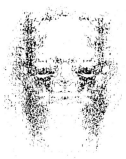

Above: a portrait of New Orleans' father of jazz King Oliver for Wire (xerography). Left: portrait of Grandmaster Flash, commissioned by New Musical Express for the release of his hit "White Lines". It was done, says Wright, "in table salt on black paper"

Below, left: Wright fulfilled a longtime ambition when he designed this deck for Slam City Skates (acrylic). Right, above and below: covers for The Catalogue, the publication of independent label Rough Trade Records

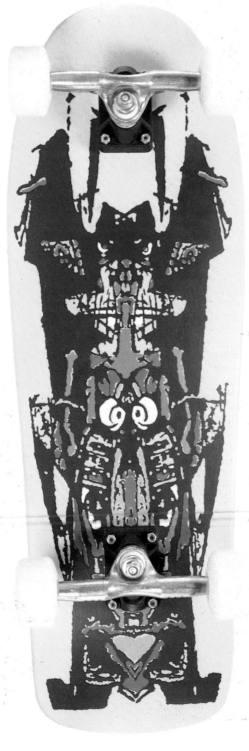

Left: a portrait of mysterious jazz maestro Sun Ra (inks on breadboard) which was published by New Musical Express, Blitz and the Face. Below: the Melodious Funk image for a T-shirt by Straight No Chaser (Apple Macintosh)

Far left: when it could not afford the repro fee for his extant photographs, Wire magazine commissioned this portrait of blues great Robert Johnson. For legal reasons Wright's portrait could not look "too much" like the musician. But, working from the forbidden image, he came up with this xerographed Rorschach of music's most mysterious legend. It accompanied an article by critic Greil Marcus

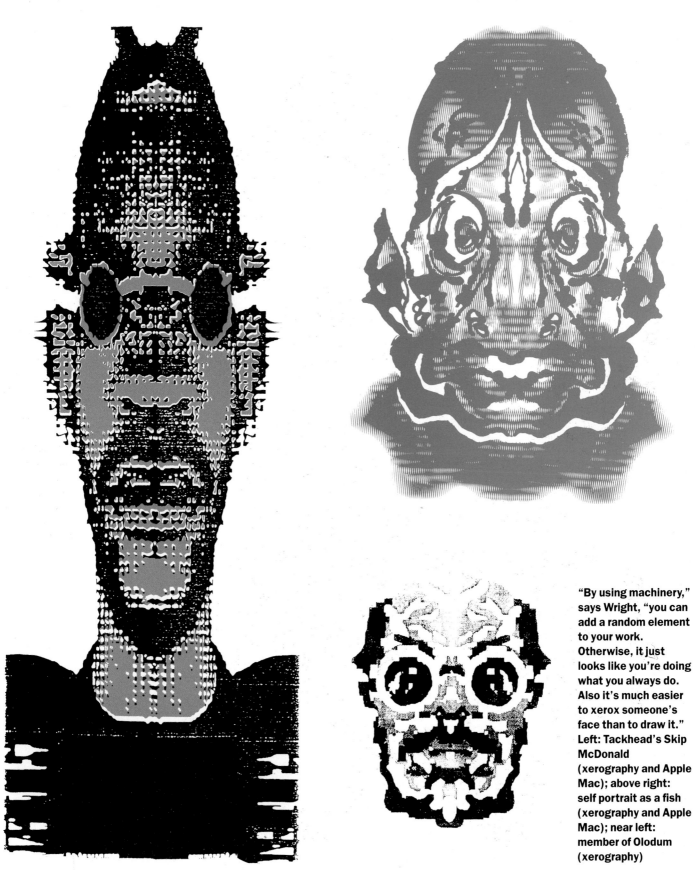

"By using machinery," says Wright, "you can add a random element to your work. Otherwise, it just looks like you're doing what you always do. Also it's much easier to xerox someone's face than to draw it."
Left: Tackhead's Skip McDonald (xerography and Apple Mac); above right: self portrait as a fish (xerography and Apple Mac); near left: member of Olodum (xerography)

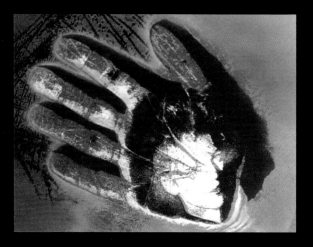

"Use the technology," says this designer. "Then take it out of your computer and back to the screenprinting table or xerox machine." Opposite page: selections from 26 portraits of South Bank Show subjects commissioned by London Weekend Television (xerography and Quantel computer). This page: logo for a Consuming Passions article in Arena magazine

Paul Elliman
Iconic Imagery

To graphic designer Paul Elliman the mobile outlook of dancefloor design comes naturally; he has never stayed put in any one place for long. "I went to a different school every year, mostly in towns around Liverpool. My last year in school, we moved to Portsmouth - right at the height of punk." There, Elliman's art teacher took him to see the Clash. But when he saw the Sex Pistols, it was 6,000 miles away - in San Francisco.

"My parents moved to America. In England, I was too young for punk. But when I got to America, I was right there - and it was all brand-new." While the Elliman family settled in San Jose, California, Paul found work in a photographic lab. He learned colour processing alongside Mexican teens who worshipped "lowrider" cars. But within two years, he was back in England at Portsmouth Polytechnic. "I did two years there - one in sociology, the next an art foundation." He then dropped out and set off to rejoin his family.

"I took a portfolio of paintings, thinking I would get work as an illustrator. And I did, in San Francisco, on a magazine called City Sports. We got on really well, so they started to train me in rudimentary production skills: pasteup, printing, a bit of type. I didn't learn a lot. But I discovered I did have opinions about magazine design." Back in England in 1984, Elliman took a layout job at London weekly City Limits. He was hired the same day - for an identical job - as his friend Phil Bicker, who later became Art Director of The Face.

The job at City Limits led Elliman into the jazz magazine Wire; and by 1986 he had become its Design Director. Both in and outside the UK his work at the slim, small-circulation mag was noticed by innumerable designers, photographers and graphic artists. It won him as a judge for the 1988 Design & Art Direction Award (for Editorial and Book Design). And it spawned a broad spectrum of "homages": from Robert Newman's design of New York's Village Voice Jazz Supplements to the 1989 re-design of IPC's Woman's Journal in Britain.

WIRE

ISSUE 48 FEBRUARY 1988 £1.40 $4.00

Jazz Age:
Billie Holiday
photographed by
Herman Leonard,
conversation with
Joe Henderson,
the story of
King Oliver.

ABCDEFGHIJKLMN

Above: Wire magazine cover and, right, spread featuring the work of famous jazz photographer Herman Leonard. Elliman was introduced to Leonard by another great jazz lensman, Marc Bicker

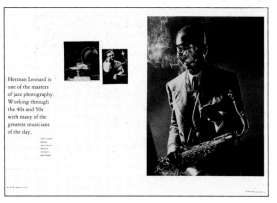

Herman Leonard is one of the masters of jazz photography. Working through the 40s and 50s with many of the greatest musicians of the day,

Players: On these pages
we present some of the
men and women who
have helped to shape
Britain's jazz and new
music over the course of
Wire's 50 issues.

ANNIE WHITEHEAD appeared on
the cover of issue 14. A trombonist and composer with records of
her own, Annie has lately been
working with James Blood Ulmer
and is currently reviving her own
band. Photo by PETER ANDERSON.

WIRE MAGAZINE 17

Players

ROLAND PERRIN is a London-based pianist and leader of
the group Evidence. A composer steeped in the spirits of
Monk and Ellington, his
music offers a synthesis of
many influences.. Roland
will be featured in a future
issue. Photo by JENNY
ANDERSON.

PHIL DURRANT is
a violinist and
trombonist work-
ing primarily in
improvisation. His trio record with John
Russell and John Butcher is reviewed
this month; he has also appeared on two
recent compilations of House music.
Photo by NEIL DRABBLE.

STEVE WILLIAMSON,
tenor and soprano saxo-
phone, was featured in
issue 16. He has finally
signed a record contract,
for Antilles, and his first
LP under his own name is
due later this year. Photo
by BRUCE RAE.

16 WIRE MAGAZINE

Above: page spreads from Wire. Above, far right: Steve Williamson photographed by Bruce Rae. Below: regular column by Wire's Paris correspondent Mike Zwerin. Right, top: photograph of Hornweb by Simon Durrant; right, bottom: photograph of Steve Arguelles by Robert Torbert

feel

LIKE A SAX

MACHINE

A foursquare set of hormones
from Sheffield

THE HORNWEB is a Saxophone Quartet consists of four people who play
saxophones, but let your preconceptions run there. It is not a classical ensemble
dedicated to the accurate rendering of a single composer's score, nor is it a jazz
group...

SAXOPHONE
AND DRUMS
KEEP IT IN THE
FAMILY

Schizzed Out in the

Mike Zwerin in NYC talks to guitarist

Apple: Drugs can still make

Mike Stern and altoist Frank

you famous — but only

Morgan, two survivors of a fatal attraction.

if you kick the habit.

NEW YORK: bouncing down Park Avenue South trying to catch ten
green lights, the taxi driver said he was writing a book about the history of "The Great
American (unprintable act)", which he traces back to the French influence on our
doughboys during World War I. I gave him $4 for the ride and $2 for the rap and got
out in front of 55 Christopher Street.
    The 55 Bar used to be called a hospital. New York's creative elite like the poet
Delmore Schwartz and Paul Desmond drank themselves to death in that dive. Now the
enthralled audience listening to a hard-driving Mike Stern worship Wes Montgomery,
Jimi Hendrix and John Coltrane made it seem more like a temple.
    Stern had been much more rocky during his three years with Miles Davis — on more
than one level. He was sniffing what he calls "paragraphs" rather than lines of cocaine

WIRE MAGAZINE 17

91

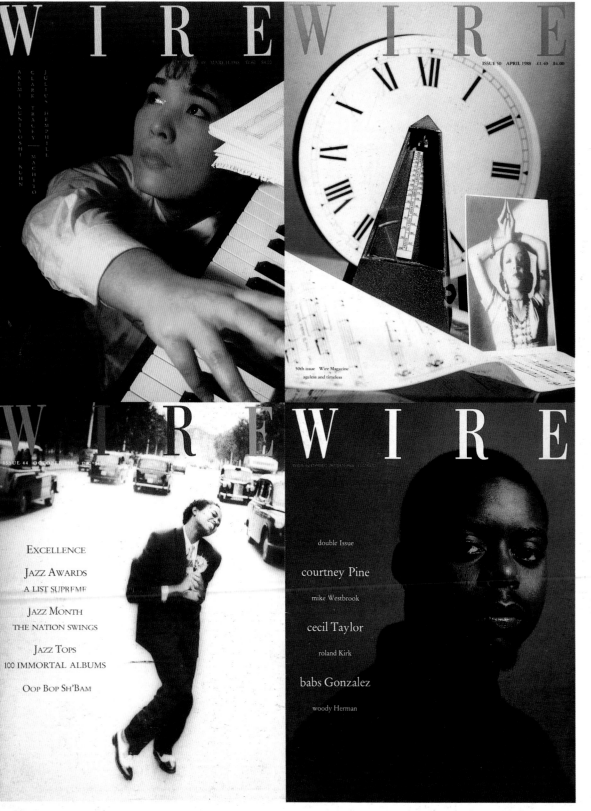

Covers for Wire magazine, "a strong identity aiming straight for the reader". They include, top left: pianist Akemi Kunyoshi-Kuhn Top right: a cover for the magazine's 50th issue (devised around the slogan Ageless and Timeless). Bottom, left: cover promoting the National Jazz Awards.The colours used here on the magazine's logo pay homage to the design of a classic jazz album, John Coltrane's Ascension. Bottom, right: portrait shot of Courtney Pine by Mark Lewis

Directly below: for the "Tokyo-dori" series now being published as a book, Elliman used his own photographs

BLACK BY POPULAR DEMAND

Asian Voices, British Lives

Black by popular DEMAND

Black and Blue: Black Women in Blues & Jazz

BLACK By Popular Demand

Black From The Past

Early Cinema

VOLUME I

Primitives and Pioneers

LUMIERE/Sortie d'usine (1895) Repas de Bébé (1895) Demolition d'un mur (1895) Le jardinier et le petit espiegle. (1895) Arrivée des Congressistes à Neuville-sur Saône (1895) Arrivée d'un train en gare à La Ciotat (1895) Partie d'ecarte (1895) Barque sortant du port (1895) Leaving Jerusalem By Railway (1896) Bataille de Boules de Neige (1896) Pompiers à Lyon. (c1896) Niagara (1897) Spanish Bullfight (1900) MELIES/Voyage à travers l'impossible (1904) ACRES/ Rough Sea at Dover (1895) R.W.PAUL/ Come Along Doll (1898) The Derby (1896) The Countryman and the Cinematograph (1901) A Chess Dispute (1903) Extraordinary Cab Accident (1903) Buy Your Own Cherries (1904) The (?) Motorist (1906) GEORGE ALBERT SMITH/The Miller and the Sweep (1898) The Kiss in the Tunnel (1899) Let Me Dream Again, (1900)

Piano accompaniment: Neil Brand
Voiceover: Charles Jameson
Commentary by: Barry Salt
Design: Paul Elliman

Approximate running time 70 mins

Grandma's Reading Glass (1900) As Seen Through a Telescope (1900) Sick Kitten (1903) Mary Jane's Mishap (1903) SHEFFIELD PHOTO COMPANY/Daring Daylight Burglary (1903) HAGGAR AND SONS/Desperate Poaching Affray (1903) BAMFORTH AND CO. LTD./The Kiss in the Tunnel (1899) Ladies Skirts Nailed to a Fence (c1900) The Bitter Bit (1900) Rough Sea (c1900) WILLIAMSON'S KINEMATOGRAPH CO. LTD./ Attack on a China Mission (1900) The Big Swallow (1901?) Stop Thief (1901) Fire! (1901) An Interesting Story (1905)

Apart from the Melies title, film material supplied by the National Film Archive.

For further information, or to book a film, please contact:

Film + Video Library
British Film Institute
21 Stephen Street
London W1P 1PL
071-255 1444

bfi

Below: a January, 1989 calendar in the form of a concrete poem in asterisks

Above, top and centre: covers for two British Film Institute video compilation series. Below, directly right: a T-shirt for housing action group Shelter designed with photographer Mark Lewis

B 4

HO OM

DIN HEY

PHUT BANG

CLACQ KLANG

VAROOM CRUNCH

PACHING SCHTOSH

TEUF-TEUF N'ZEEMBO

Criticism and
Ideology
Terry Eagleton
A Study in
Marxist
Literary Theory

From Luther
to Popper
Translated by Joris De Bres
Herbert
Marcuse

Göran
Therborn
The Ideology of Power
and the Power
of Ideology

Critique Of
Dialectical
Reason
VOLUME ONE
Jean-Paul
Sartre
Theory of Practical Ensembles

Above: eye-test charts transposed for sound in an ad for hi-fi retailers the Cornflake Shop. Centre: silk-screen posters for East London Polytechnic. Right: Verso book covers

Wire's impact was strengthened by the new British jazz movement it reflected. That movement featured strong personalities - Courtney Pine, Steve Williamson, Andy Sheppard - and fresh, young ensembles with names like Loose Tubes and the Jazz Warriors. For capturing their style-consciousness, the magazine was tagged a "designer jazz journal". Yet that perception romanticised the publication's realities. Says Elliman: "People cite it as a particular example in the use of Garamond typeface. But our type was set at a little place in Kent, inherited from the first publisher. When they gave me a font list there were five choices on it. It wasn't design ideology - it was working with what I had."

Nor was the monthly an expansive operation. Its original logo, says Elliman, had been pirated from an in-house engineering mag of the same name. And the initial team of photographers were buffs, who "took a few snaps whenever they attended concerts". What kept Elliman going, as he laid out every page himself? "I taught myself through those limitations. Became familiar with the typeface, then learned all the other rules - like composition and scale. I had never studied design, and this was my first real job."

What came first was ideas: "It was like making a genre film. In a naive way, a strong reference was my imagined idea of Cahiers du Cinema in the '50s or '60s, when the contributors included Godard and Truffaut. Guys who were saying French film was dead, but who then went on to transform it."

Another linchpin concern was strong, classic photography. "That was a matter," says Elliman, "of giving these musicians the degree of respect they deserved. Again, it's a thing of genre. If you know what you're after, you go for the right person. Even if it's a fashion photographer who'll be a little difficult. None of the photographers I used at Wire were working fulltime in music. I did inherit, through the Editor (ex-New Musical Express staffer Richard Cook), some who were. And I liked their work very much. But I started to discard them, because I needed the Wire to go somewhere fresh." Instead, he recruited lensmen like Mark Lewis, then shooting fashion for Iain R Webb at Blitz, and jazz-photography great Herman Leonard - an American living quietly in London.

His sense of the possible, says Elliman, came from magazines he saw in America: New West, San Francisco's Boulevards and City; Chicago's Fetish, Los Angeles's legendary WET. "They convinced me that an editorial framework is conducive to the best creative work: illustration, photography, typography. And all of them were strong on teamwork. That's easier to build on non-mainstream magazines. They're not controlled by market forces and they need personality."

For Elliman, a clear visual identity is tied to iconic images. "Always, for me, one image says it - whether it's the Wire Jazz Awards or The Holborn Centre for Performing Arts. Whether you shoot three Polaroids or ten rolls of film. But that's an instinctive thing; you'll never find statistics fully to back it up."

After almost two years, Elliman left Wire. And, after six months doing weekly covers for London's City Limits, he set off on a long-planned trip around Japan. There, in tandem with two other designers, he published a one-off magazine and a book of silk-screen prints. In January 1990, he helped launch Osaka arts glossy Meets Regional (a "Japanese Time Out", for which he still designs every cover). He then moved on again - travelling to California, Germany, Portugal. "I worked for a number of clients in all these different places. But what I really enjoyed while travelling was transmitting Box Space."

Box Space is Elliman's UK-based electronic mail magazine. Produced on Facsimile machines, modems and computers, its format and language are completely flexible: "It's a great way for people in different places to work together." At the end of his two-year travels, West Germany's Kunst published his "electronic retrospective". But for now, says the designer, he's content to channel his urge to roam through technology.

"I'm always drawn back to the amount of talent in Britain," says Elliman. "I'm not into that thing of 'doing it for the prestige' - which is the only way a lot of young British work sees publication. That's bullshit, and every photographer, painter and designer knows it. What people will do it for, however, is the energy. Here, for the past five years, there's been more and more of that."

The Cornflake Shop

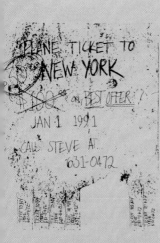

Above: New Year's card for the Cornflake Shop, after a flyposter torn off a San Francisco wall

Above: cover of a Systems Manual for the Cornflake Shop (designed with Moira Bogue); below, print ads: onomatopoeic words used to twin a word's literal sense with its sound

At The Cornflake Shop we sell a selection of the world's finest Hi Fi equipment – from £400 record playing systems to complete round-the-house remote controlled multi room systems. Come to The Cornflake Shop. You'll find us friendly, helpful, knowledgeable and honest!

The Cornflake Shop
37 Windmill Street London W1P 1HH
071 631 0472 Fax 071 436 7165

At The Cornflake Shop we sell a selection of the world's finest Hi Fi equipment – from £400 record playing systems to complete round-the-house remote controlled multi room systems. Come to The Cornflake Shop. You'll find us friendly, helpful, knowledgeable and honest!

The Cornflake Shop
37 Windmill Street London W1P 1HH
071 631 0472 Fax 071 436 7165

D I N
D
A
N

At The Cornflake Shop we sell a selection of the world's finest Hi Fi equipment – from £400 record playing systems to complete round-the-house remote controlled multi room systems. Come to The Cornflake Shop. You'll find us friendly, helpful, knowledgeable and honest!

The Cornflake Shop
37 Windmill Street London W1P 1HH
071 631 0472 Fax 071 436 7165

WE ALWAYS FIND SOMETHING EH DIDI TO GIVE US THE IMPRESSION WE EXIST

Above: title page of a book of photos published by Newcastle's Northern Stage Company

Right: logo for Box Space (designed with Peter Miles)

BOX SPACE

Consisting of banners, sculpture, painted floorboards and projections, club art is big, loud and able to be dismantled. In tandem with handouts, membership cards and the occasional print ad, artists like Georgiou attempt to give each club a separate visual ambiance

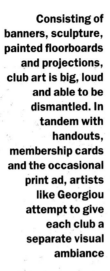

Top, across from left: Sin, RAW, The Milk Bar; bottom, across from left: RAW, The Milk Bar, RAW

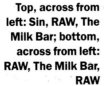

Below: handouts by Georgiou for club entrepreneur Danny Rampling, at West London's Subterania venue (bottom) and (top) the flyer for Shoom, one of the dancefloor's most famous designs

George Georgiou
Moveable Feasts

George Georgiou is experienced at architecting ambiance: since 1985, he has designed and painted more than 2,000 square metres of canvas and almost as much 8'x4' plyboard. These cloths and boards transformed old-fashioned pubs and nondescript clubrooms into some of London's most legendary nightspots: hangouts with names like RAW, Special Branch, Sin, Shoom, the Milk Bar, Alphabet City. Their flyers, posters and membership cards have also been Georgiou's doing - including inventive schemes like voice cassettes, wooden toys and handouts printed on perspex.

By trade an interior designer, Georgiou was recruited to clubland by entrepreneur Oliver Peyton (a classmate at Leicester Polytechnic). Peyton's first club, publicised by Georgiou's flyers, was called BB Crop - after the "Borstal Boy" haircut - and took place in Tisbury Court, Soho, in 1985. That autumn, Peyton opened RAW in the Tottenham Court Road YMCA - and Georgiou again handled his PR. The club's flyers were stuffed, like fortune cookies, into 10,000 medicine capsules. Georgiou also painted the boards which, re-assembled every week, constituted the RAW dancefloor.

By early '86, RAW had soared in popularity, and Peyton decided to completely re-design it. Though Christos Tolleros had painted the original canvas walls, Peyton asked Georgiou to visualise his new decor. By this time, the designer had teamed up with Hornsey College colleague Tony Papaloizou to form a club design team they called "General Practice".

"We worked every night after our day jobs," says Georgiou, "out of a warehouse near Blackfriars Bridge. Literally, it was paint-by-numbers: we had a team of six painters who followed me as I drew. The whole RAW scheme took less than a month. With clubs it's always like that - always rush, rush."

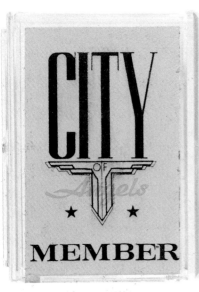

RAW schooled Georgiou in the emerging design requirements of London's one-night clubs. "The thing about canvas and banners," he says, "is they could change an atmosphere completely. But you had to remember what you can see inside a club; when it's packed, everything is happening above head height. Also, there are very few lights - so subtleties will be lost." Instead, Georgiou went for bright colours and a bold graphic style. And he made sure decor could be taken apart and stored at the end of each evening.

RAW brought General Practice steady work, which ranged from funky domestic commissions to flyers and banners for other clubs. It also introduced Georgiou to a stream of clubland entrepreneurs. By the spring of 1986, he was working for DJ Nicky Holloway, redesigning a Royal Oak pub for Holloway's one nighter Special Branch. "Nicky had invited me to his 'Do At the Zoo' and I couldn't believe it. He had 12,000 people getting down, inside London Zoo! Racially, it was very mixed. And he had all sorts of music: jazz, hip-hop, rare grooves. . . . From RAW I was used to a Soho crowd. But Nicky's punters really came for the music and the scene. What people wore didn't really matter so much to them."

After he did banners for a Holloway 'All-Dayer' - his last job as half of General Practice - Georgiou began the new partnership. "Nicky did clubs at Lords Cricket Ground, at Chichester Caves, at the

Natural History Museum. But what he really wanted was to get a foot in the West End." By Christmas '88, he got it - through taking over Charing Cross Road's massive Astoria Theatre for "Sin". And Georgiou got big-time, big-league decoration work.

Before that could happen, however, came the Shoom club and Acid house. "Danny Rampling was Nicky's best mate, and so I already knew him," says Georgiou. "When he set up Shoom, he asked me for a logo, flyers, banners." Rampling specified the Smiley face for his handouts. But Georgiou had the idea to show those Smileys tumbling down, like a cascade of then-popular pills. He drew all the Shoom banners - and Mr and Mrs Rampling painted them.

By this time, RAW had mutated into City of Angels: a tony, Sloane-y club serving pricey Japanese beer. Georgiou handled its flyers and its micro-cassette "Membership Cards". "But I was still working full-time," he says. "And all my club work had to be done outside studio hours." His 'day work' ranged from interiors for Monty Python star Terry Gilliam's house to fancy downtown shopping sites in Soho's Trocadero. But, by the end of 1989, club work helped enable Georgiou to go completely freelance.

"I learned a lot of entrepreneurial tricks from the club-runners," he says today. "Nicky, for instance, was really together from very early on. He had his little computer, his 17,000-name mailing list. He

used to give beer-and-crisp parties and we'd all stuff envelopes together."

At the beginning of 1990, Holloway asked Georgiou to decorate a new club, the Milk Bar. The designer, who had in the meantime run a club of his own (The Last Temptation), decided to go for a post-Acid vibe. "I would liked to have done murals on the walls, with ultraviolet paint. But Acid killed off that idea. When we were planning the Milk Bar, the scene was in limbo. But the Last Temptation had part of the post-Acid religious vibe - and it was the first all-white colour scheme I'd used.

"So I fought tooth-and-nail to do the Milk Bar in white drapes. I wanted it clean and simple, with a back-to-the-warehouse feel."

Adding bright-coloured blocks for sitting and a platform to serve as the dancefloor, Georgiou took the rundown, back-alley site and gave Nicky Holloway another thriving venue. Just as Georgiou's banners pointed early clubbers towards portable art, his early-'90s designs return clubland to basic concerns: good sounds, good vibes, good times.

"That's the lesson of the dancefloor," he says. "You don't need fancy stuff. By the summer of '89, all these flyers were appearing in full colour, printed on both sides - very exotic, very elaborate and Roger Dean. And people were charging £25, £30 for a night. Maybe you can do that, but you shouldn't."

Most designers were friends with their clients, and partnerships could run and run. For Nicky Holloway, Georgiou came up with ticket after ticket: each aimed at broadening the club runner's milleu. Above: Special Branch, out in the suburbs; right: Sin, in the West End. Below, left: RAW; below right: The Milk Bar, both trendy in-town sites

157 CHARING CROSS RD. LONDON WC2

FRIDAYS & SATURDAYS

RAW/CITY OF ANGELS

88

£8 BEFORE 10·30 £10 AFTER — BEDFORD AVE,WC1

NEW YEARS EVE PARTY

THE BASEMENT 12 SUTTON ROW (OFF SOHO SQUARE)

THE MILK BAR

PRESENTS

To musicians as much as to gallery-owners, Fiona Hawthorne is a more than familiar face. Usually, this artist-designer is drawing as they play - whatever the size of the venue or the listening audience. Sketches of Big Nights Out, of rehearsals and one-off concerts, have become popular facets of Hawthorne's regular shows. And she tries to secure exhibition space which operates in a populist mode: cafes, theatre galleries, jazz events.

Married to trumpeter Colin Salmon, Hawthorne is known as the artist who successfully caught the emergence of Britain's young jazz scene. (In 1989, when Jazz-FM was launched, much of the station's advertising was done in a knockoff Hawthorne style.) But her love of jazz as the live moment dates from an unusual background.

Born in Northern Ireland, Hawthorne spent her childhood in Hong Kong - and, before art college in London, she attended Atlantic College in Wales. "From an early age," she says, "I went to school in a very mixed culture: with people of all races, all colours, all kinds of language skills. I wasn't part of any majority. So I feel comfortable in mixed atmospheres."

Music played a large part in her stimulating childhood - and so did drawing from life. "I've drawn as long as I can remember. When we travelled, mum kept my sketchbook in her bag. Then when we were bored, when there were delays, my sister and brother and I would draw. We drew on the tablecloths of restaurants, on airport floors, on walls."

For Hawthorne, drawing became "pure pleasure. I loved it like other kids get into reading or playing with favourite toys." Now, she says, she regrets any period of not drawing and holidays or gigs are events she keenly anticipates. "I love it when Colin is due to play. I know I'll go along and I'll get lots of drawing in."

From the age of 16 to 19, Hawthorne financed her own travels with both drawing and music. "I played tin whistle, Irish music, and used to go busking round Europe with friends. When I wasn't playing, I

Above, left: videocassette cover commemorating London's first Soho Jazz Festival; above, right: design for the re-release of a film classic. Centre: steel drummers at West London's Notting Hill Carnival. Below: album cover for go-go star Chuck Brown. Opposite page: commissioned painting celebrating the Blue Note jazz label

CHUCK BROWN and the SOUL SEARCHERS

LIVE - D.C. BUMPIN' Y'ALL

Above: portrait of Island Records star Courtney Pine

Above: from commissioned portfolio of wedding sketches

used to draw. We'd sell the drawings I did. And I financed every holiday like that."

Relocated in London for college, she moved to Ladbroke Grove: an area with genial street life and vivid musical ties. "Notting Hill Carnival blew me away, epecially the West Indian steel bands. 'Cause the players are so relaxed, yet everything's moving in rhythm. The carriage sways and the music carries and the kids laugh and wave. I got infatuated with drawing Carnival scenes."

She felt the same way towards jazz - and the young British players who emerged around 1985. "I've always loved drawing live music. When somebody's playing out, when they've got the right attitude, it speaks directly to you; it inspires you. I went to see Courtney Pine very early on, at Bay 63. And, although I didn't sketch him, I vividly remember storing what he looked like in my mind. Just the shape of him, and the glint of the sax."

Hawthorne met her husband through her own attraction to jazz. Now, with daughter Sasha, they comprise an artistic team: Salmon plays and Fiona draws. Hawthorne has come to view how she

works as musical in its own way. "When music plays, and it's something to do with real self-expression, somehow you draw in tune with that. When there's a real good solo, I'll often come out with a really nice drawing. I don't spend long on any one thing; I just fill a sketchbook out of one session. And out of that sketchbook I might do two or three drawings that actually hit."

She hasn't really worked out any great theory about it, "but somewhere there's a real link with jazz and my kind of drawing. A lot of my best work over the past few years has been of jazz people playing." The musicians themselves agree. Young jazz stars like Pine and Cleveland Watkiss request her for portraits and sleeve art, just as Britain's Channel Four has commissioned Hawthorne's art to enhance programmes like Big World Cafe and Jazz Diary.

But Hawthorne does not confine her investigation of the live moment to music. In addition to commercial work, she draws weddings, street life, action portraits. Thames TV sent her back to Hong Kong, where she spent long days

drawing inside the notorious Walled City. But, whatever the venue, Hawthorne produces work which boasts strong dynamics and a genuine rhythmic impulse. "The jobs I like the most," she says, "all require reportage: going and drawing people inside their own atmosphere. I love that, I'm inspired by what's happening in front of me."

As with most creators attracted to dancefloor culture, the word "community" often recurs when Hawthorne speaks of her work. "One of the interesting things is seeing young Britain change its ideas about what 'community' means.

"At college," Hawthorne says "students used to look at my work and say, 'You draw Chinese people, black people, Asians - don't you feel people are going to think you're racist?' I was a little bemused by this, because they were only seeing one thing. What actually attracts me is the nature of the event. And some of the most vibrant, significant, drawable performers in Britain are black. Maybe in the art world not everyone has made that discovery. But now I know what they really can't see is how their country has changed."

Left: the late jazz drummer Art Blakey, one of nine artists' portraits commissioned for the cover of "Jazz At Ronnie's", a compilation featuring three decades at the central London jazz venue

Above, left: American saxophonist Jean Touissant playing in North London's Jazz Cafe. Right: portrait of trumpet great Dizzy Gillespie, for the video release of his 1980 concert in Havana

London amusement clubbing

Paul Smith

'80年代が幕を
閉じようとしている今、
かつてのロンドンの
クラブ・カルチャーは
主流ではなくなり、
10年間築いてきた
スタイルは最早、
死んでしまったという
専門家さえいる。
新しい時代が
始まったのだ。
この特集では、
クラブ、バー、そして
先端の時代感覚を
楽しむために
人が集まる場所
いわば文化の坩堝を
中心にロンドンの街を
ガイドする。
紹介するのはポール・
ブラッドショー。
モダンで拍手喝采の
ワールド・ジャズ・
ジャイブ・マガジン
「ストレート・ノー・
チェイサー」誌
編集人兼発行人である。

ロンドン・アミューズメント・クラビング

Opposite page, left: magazine insert on the London club scene for Tokyo's Meets Regional magazine. Right: logo for Incognito a band on Talking Loud records; centre, compact disc publicising the label's new acts for 1990. Bottom: sleeve for Island Records' CFM Band ("Jazz It Up"), featuring art by Ian Wright

incognito

Ian Swift
Northern Soul

Raised in the small town of Huyton, 15 minutes from Liverpool, Ian Swift is keen on the Northern virtues of hard work, patience and thrift. From the summer of 1986 through the summer of 1990, he served a long apprenticeship as a style press Junior Designer - first on The Face, then on Arena. "I didn't go out in the world and just do it; really, I was quite patient. But I didn't make tea or anything, either. From the start I got my pages and sections to design."

The steady, reliable work was important in other ways, says Swift. "Learning production, typography, having to deal with printers: that's the side of this industry you only learn by experience. Plus, I was only 21. I was learning to deal with people as well."

For two years he didn't do anything "particularly wonderful". But having security, learning the trade, was of paramount importance. "I like security, with me that's a very big thing. Because my mum died when I was 7, my father when I was 16. Since I lived like that, I learned to sort things out on me own."

Ian Swift's enjoyment of dancefloor culture, he says, has less to do with the style press than with deep Merseyside roots. "When I was growing up there, the place was very rich. You had Echo and the Bunnymen and that lot coming through really strong; Probe the Record shop; Madness at the Empire. Anything which happens there gets incredible popular support. When John Lennon died, I remember going to town - and the streets were filled with hundreds of people, just walkin' around payin' homage. We stayed there all night, because the city just came alive."

Originally, says Swift, he was actually "a bit of a painter". Then, on his foundation course, "a tutor stuck copies of Blitz and New Sounds, New Styles under my nose and said, 'Look at these!' It came at just the right time for me. I loved all that

photocopying, juxtaposing and jigglin' round of typefaces. The way they combined all these faces which wouldn't normally go together."

Swift also discovered a deep love for technology - when he came upon the Apple Mac during his third year at Manchester. By this time, he was designing Fresh, an inter-departmental graphic magazine founded by designer Dave Crow (now Art Director at Island Records). "We had got hold of a couple of Macs, so I used them to produce the mag and I found it brilliant. It just seemed so integrated. So much design is still type on one side and image on the other."

Two months before Swift left college, tutor Pam Shenck asked Neville Brody up from London - to lecture on The Face. After his talk, Brody saw every student's work: in alphabetical order, which meant that Swift was last. "But, he loved my stuff! He wrote out his number in London and told me to give him a bell. Of course, it took me two weeks to actually track him down." During that fortnight, Malcolm Garrett also visited Manchester Poly; as an emissary of Factory Records' 10th Summer Anniversary. "At that stage," says Swift, "I wasn't putting all my eggs in one basket. So, I was sittin' there showing Malcolm my stuff. And just as I said, 'Any chance of some work?', the telephone next to

me rang." On the line was Neville Brody - offering Swift a job.

Eighteen months after joining The Face and, subsequently, Arena, Swift joined Neville Brody's studio. He continued working on Arena, and in spring 1990, he was made its Art Director. "Being at Neville's was great," he says. "It got me doing so many things: catalogues, logos, posters. Then Straight No Chaser came along. I knew Neil [Spencer] and Paul [Bradshaw] were working on it," says Swift of the slick jazz fanzine. "I also knew it was all being done on an Apple Mac. One day, Neil mentioned that all they lacked was a fulltime designer - so I volunteered." Much of Swift's other work, such as the design of Phonogram's Talking Loud dancefloor label (the projects of DJ Gilles Peterson), has come from the Chaser connection. And, in May 1990, i-D Art Editor Stephen Male cited its design when he chose Ian Swift for a Creative Direction 'Class of 1990' Award.

Swift sees computer technology and dancefloor culture as analogous. "It's a language of sound, image and reference. And, among contemporary designers who understand one another, a similar language is getting under way. Putting everything into one symbol - whether it's a logo or a Smiley face - is like computer-compatibility. It's another

language, developing among people on the same wavelength."

Most of the dancefloor designers, says Swift, know each other's work ("even if we don't know each other's names"). "I'm not entirely a clubber type, but I know what's goin' on. I also know who's really out there, whose work can encapsulate a style. For instance, I'll go and buy new trainers. Then I pick up a club handout and - there they are. Chris Long has captured them, with a couple of little brushstrokes."

Swift prefers the routine of work, spiced with such discoveries, to the nurturing of image. "Your ego shouldn't come first. That leads to inappropriate choices; you tend to try anything, just because you want to do it. Sometimes what's required is just to be very straight and informative." For those reasons, he says he also prefers a tight brief. "I like to know what the person really wants. Because, in the end, anything else will only cause grief."

The future? "I want to get more image into my work, I like the idea of combining type and image in a different way. I've now got two magazines to do: Chaser and Arena. So I just want to produce good, interesting work. But I won't go into TV or film - I'm a two-dimensional kind of guy!"

Opposite page, top: logos from jazz fanzine Straight No Chaser. Bottom, this page: Straight No Chaser spreads.
Swift: "The attempt is to use photographs to their maximum potential, but link them with strong typography
in the jazz and Blue Note design traditions."

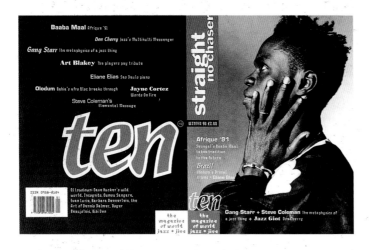

Left: CD inlay for Japanese station Mirage Super Top Wave; above: covers from the same fanzine

DREAM WARRIORS

my definition of
a boombastic
jazz style

young disciples mixes

the next definition ● soul vendor dub ● all blues

A 12" sleeve for the Young Disciples' remix of a chart hit by Canada's Dream Warriors

Shake and Fingerpop Productions Present

INNER CITY BLUES

10pm till 3am
£6 Admission
Sat 9th Feb 91
At the
ADI Centre
281 Lambeth Rd
S.E.1

Norman Jay
Musiquarium
Bass Clef-
Shake and Finger
Gilles Peterson
The Fez-
Talkin Loud an
Saying Someth

"Makin' you wanna holler and hold your hands up in the air"

At **The Shack**, Tisbury Court (Off Wardour St, Opp Old Compton St) 9pm -3am.

* DJ'S - **Nick** Night In Havana **Antonio** Straight No Chaser **Nigel** Eastsides Finest **Peter Yang** WLIB 92.4 FM

toward tomorrows underground

Jazz attak

Saturday £5:00 before 10pm. £7:00 thereafter

Talkin Loud & Saying Something 3rd Anniversary meets Straight No Chaser to present

Dave Valentin Quintet
Numero Uno Latin Jazz flautist - 4pm
The Courtney Pine All Stars
Jam session stylee - 7pm
Kid Frost + Jalal + Galliano
DJs Gilles Peterson & Patrick Forge

Sunday, 2nd December, 1990. 1am to 9pm Dingwalls Camden Lock, NW1 (071 267 4967) £7 on Door (£5 for members)

jazz/hip hop

featuring **gilles peterson** and brother **marco**   fortnightly **sat 27th oct**/
10th nov/
8th dec/
22nd dec

Controversy

at the underworld   £5 before **11pm** £6 after **174** camden high st **NW1**

Jazz/Hip Hop
Gilles Peterson
Patrick Forge
Kevin Beadle

the Fez

Fridays at the Starlight Club
Gt Western Hotel
Praed st, London W2
£6 10.30pm till late

Opposite page: tickets designed to give some impression of what each club will be like. This page, far left: flyer for The Fez, reflecting the club's reputation by a deliberate reference to 1960s graphics. Left top, left below and below right: logos for businesses (all designed on the Apple MacIntosh computer)

jazz 90

9pm till late

£3.50 with this leaflet

On : Sat 24th Feb 1990 At : The Emerald Centre, Hammersmith (On the roundabout next to the tube st) Music : Down the line ....Hard Core DJ's : Sylvester and Gilles Peterson.

Above: a flyer for the one-nighter event Jazz 90. Claims Ian Swift: "This is how the logo for Jazz-FM (the London radio station licensed in 1989) should have looked."

Basic "house bag" (promotional sleeve) designed for Phonogram Records' Talking Loud subsidiary, toying with symbols of copyright to reflect the use of sampling and mixing within that label's product

113

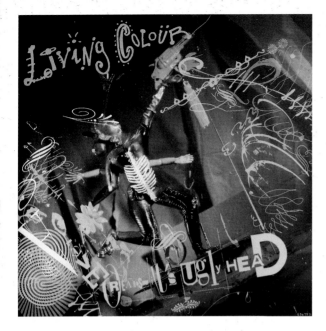

Below: the designers scramble toys, cultural iconographies and religious references in 3-D sculptures like this one for a Living Colour sleeve

Opposite page: Thunderjockeys John England, top, and Graham Elliott, below, bring the party atmosphere to work. Here, they are in a studio they built as a set for their MTV press shots. Left: a 12" sleeve for Living Colour. Below right: the Thunderjockeys' format for Videographic magazine (1989-1990)

VIDEOGRAPHIC

The Thunderjockeys
Graphics A Go - Go

Together since they met at the Royal College of Art, the Thunderjockeys (Graham Elliott and John England) offer a testament to the crossover power of late-'80s chutzpah. Their work began with pure spectacle: 3-D versions of sound which incorporated sculpture, projections, computergraphics and live action. But today they can be found in a large ad agency: West London's BMP DDB Needham. Their office enjoys a unique relationship with its firm: 50 per cent of their work is composed of independent, Thunderjockeys commissions. The other half is straightforward work on agency accounts.

Though formally trained in typography and design, Elliott and England say the "loudness and optimism" which distinguish Thunderjockery came from the young London around them. "There's two scenes here," says England. "A young, kind of underground scene that the kids we know are coming from - making music or making something else. Then, there's the straight art 'business'. Not many people in that can handle those other people or even see where they're coming from. We kind of fit that category. So, really, we mediate. 'Cause we're not so involved in the scene we're going to disappear up our own arse. We're able to dip into it - then go make a milk commercial."

"Too many design groups," says Elliott, "use design as their only reference point. With bands, that's especially awful. People will do record covers who won't even go and see the band! Won't even listen to the song! They'll just knock out some roughs and put 'em on a bike."

The Thunderjocks take an opposite route; they dip into every technology going. They will do a band's sleeve and also direct its promo; design a TV station's logo as well as its onscreen graphics. They hoard cuttings and toys, sculptures and bits of type. Then they scan these into screen graphics, collage them, manipulate colour and size. In contrast to this wild world, which screams its colour and idiosyncrasy, much of their progress has come through a succession of well-placed admirers.

But they take the initiative. In 1988, fresh out of the RCA, they filled a week-long trip to Manhattan

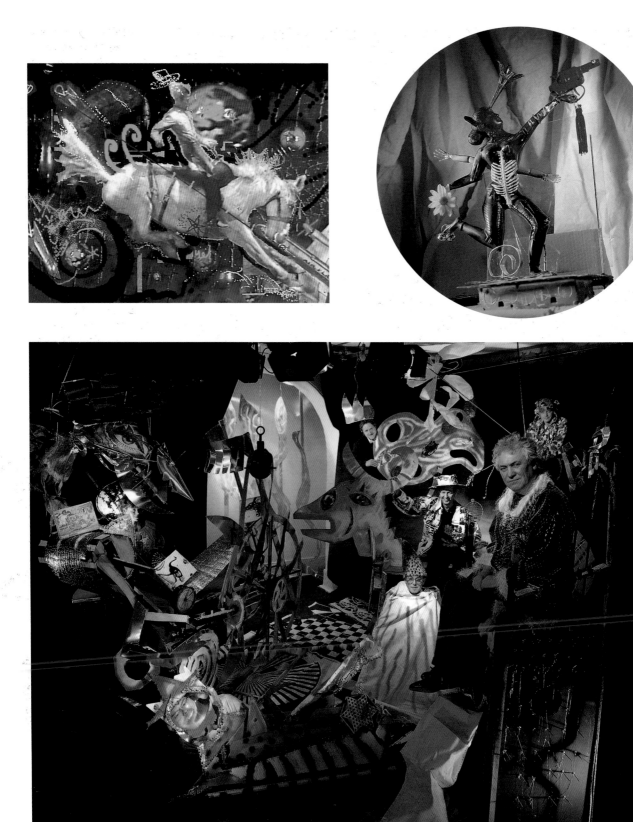

Opposite page, top left: One key to the duo's success has been their willingness to undertake promotional work, like this computer-generated image; top right: another sculpture for the second Living Colour campaign. Opposite page, bottom: To picture the jury of Design & Art Direction's 16th Annual volume of European Illustration, Elliott and England constructed both a set and costumes

This page, left: "Skittles", another portfolio piece. Below: an item from one of the pair's bulging sketchbooks

Above: part of a programme from Thunderjockey-designed event Spectacle Yummy Yummy, in Holland. Right: '89-'90, which they designed. Opposite page: spreads from the same volume

with "ten appointments a day". D & AD's Edward Booth-Clibborn sponsored them to appear at an American Illustration seminar, and the Thunderjocks used the opportunity to hustle up US clients - including Metropolis magazine and the band Living Colour.

Their work for Living Colour has ranged from badges and sleeve art to postcards and video. All vibrate with colour, noise and theatrical sass. "Our rule," says Graham Elliott, "is first, get the job. Next, decide what you really want to do. Then - figure out how."

"Living Colour", adds England, "were great because they allowed us to get computergraphics out of our system. For them, it was appropriate. Because they really were big and bold and fresh and very expansive."

In 1989, the Thunderjockeys decided to go into advertising. "Infiltrate might be a better word," says Elliott. "What happened was that, through agencies, we were giving people all these ideas. But we got a little bit tired of handing 'em over, waving goodbye and never hearing a peep again. We thought, why aren't we in there - doing those ideas."

For a date at Saatchi & Saatchi, Elliott and England appeared trailing a goat and a pet Dalmatian. "The goat shat everywhere," according to England. "And the dog

was even worse. So we got thrown out; they called the police. The next time we went in, we made sure to be ultra-straight. Saw the same guy and brought him a Hoover." The Saatchis took them on for a Christmas placement. But, within three months, they were poached by BMP.

Staff at their new HQ, they say, "find it hard to accept that we don't just do advertising." But the Thunderjocks remain believers in blurring lines and ignoring fixed roles. England considers that it's "nice to stir things up a bit. In advertising right now, it's all regurgitation. Imitations of things from the past and not ideas out of people's heads. Nothing that looks towards the future or enjoys a bit of fantasy."

"Advertising is going back on itself," says Graham Elliott. "Referring back to the ad-men's lifestyles, well away from its audience. Really, it's riddled with awful cliches. . . . All we want is to use humour, to break things down. Just bring some personality into the world of design. If it's out of a type catalogue and out of a photographer's showbook, it's always going to be squeaky-clean and fairly regimented."

Much of their work is inspired by keeping an eye on cultures around the world. "There's great stuff

everywhere," says Graham Elliott."There's toys in the streets of Mexico more creative than anything a design group will ever do. You've got to look outside yourself to find out what you're about. That was the lesson behind the whole Acid thing."

"Taking the global view is really, really important," adds England. "We try to take cultures and re-mix them, but still add something new." Whenever the duo travel, they now carry super-8 cameras - to build up a library of footage on their own. It finds a way into pop promos for figures like Carlton and Guru Josh.

The Thunderjockeys know the vision of dancefloor design is here to stay. "A lot of people say, 'How did you get by doing this sort of work?'" says Elliott. "But we've built a viable company; we now have two employees. And we kept faith with our stage name - which meant something poetic and raunchy, something to show you were after a bit of attitude. . . . We did it mostly through just working hard. But we're certainly not alone. There are lots of people like us out there. The trick is to find and use their skills, learn how to bring them in."

Editorial

Magazines et

JOURNAUX

Redaktionelle Graphix

12

Pportunity was no
ow

13

film

FilM

film

For their first trip to America, Elliott and England developed 100 computer-generated "images of desire" (opposite page, above and below), a gambit which paid off handsomely in commissions. Right: poster design for "Breakthrough", a 1988 exhibition celebrating 25 years of illustration at London's Royal College of Art. Above, right: sketchbook image

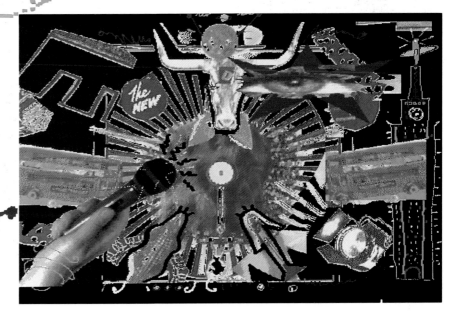

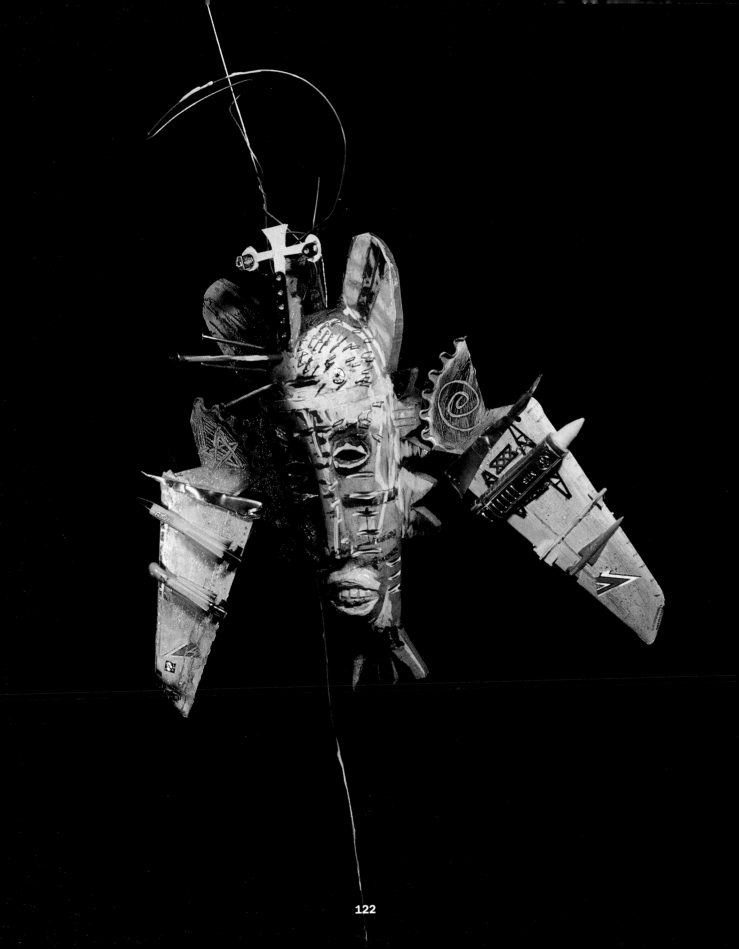

Opposite page: image for Living Colour. This page, top left: when it comes to corporate logos, dancefloor design has been to bootlegging and then back. This Thunderjockeys image for the launch of the new Polo is legitimate. Below left: LP sleeve for the Todd Terry Project's 12" "Just Wanna Dance". Below right: a sketchbook image

Mark Jackson
A Piece of the Action

"Change yourself for a Positronic future!" screams the printed page. "The technology is now available!" A slick, 40-page manifesto created on a cheap computer, Positronic magazine is a product of the streetwise science it extols. And Editor Mark Jackson distributes copies for free, leaving them on London tube seats or near bookstore exit aisles.

Graphic designer Jackson, whose Positronic project scrambles pop collage with quantum theory, works in the agitprop arts: graffiti, desktop publishing, flyers and "scratch xerox". He lumps them all together under the umbrella term strechno - for "technology fused with the street". "The basis of all my interests," says Jackson, "came out the music I listen to. I started by just doing montage. Then, for a tenner, the lady at the xerox place would let me mess around with her machines. I would mimic hip-hop techniques with a copier, try to make it scratch."

Gemini Arts, a government job scheme in Kensal Rise, London, hired Jackson to design its magazine, Borderline. But he was far more interested by a workmate named Ricky Plant. Plant was famous for two talents: expertise on a skateboard and ease with the "bunts" or Bunt-Lac graffiti spraycans. In the code-heavy world of graf, where "pieces" are "got up" or "thrown up" and "tagged" (signed), Plant operated as "Chase". Until he was caught "getting up" at Hammersmith tube station, Plant had also been a London Transport ticket collector.

With Ricky and 21-year-old Sandra Belgrave (aka Syanide), Jackson formed a legal graffiti crew, West London Pressure. Funded by West London's Tabernacle Community Centre, the trio want to formalise graffiti art, see its impact and inventiveness siphoned into other graphic spheres. "Graffiti," says Jackson, "influenced my typography more than the other way round. How to style your letters, how to build your backgrounds - you learn every aspect out on the street. You're out there every night: that's the only way you'll ever understand it."

For Jackson, xerography and collage were sampling, too. He just used visual material rather than bites of sound. Left and above: a cover for City Limits

Jackson (graffiti-tag "Contempt") and Sandra Belgrave (graffiti-tag "Syanide") in their West London squat with its customised walls. From here, they run a grafitti design service. Below: graffiti-influenced club ticket for Sweet To the Bone, designed by Jackson

Jackson has set out to translate the energies of taggers like Plant and Belgrave into new dimensions: an orbit of ozone-friendly sprayguns and Situationist cheek. His mission has called for both organisation (seeking commissions from clubs, pubs and shops, sorting out grants, hustling materials) and technical groundwork. "To do legal graf," he says, "we learn what undercoats and over-paints to use; how many coats; eggshell or gloss."

Jackson's aims have been supported by the Tabernacle's David Curtis, who has sponsored both strechno and graffiti exhibitions. "A whole range of new techniques and skills are being invented here," says Curtis. "The sort of results they're achieving are quite unique. And they should be given respect by some of the powers-that-be." Italian publishing house Stanter Alta Nativa agrees. During 1989, it took Jackson and other spraycan stylists on two week-long European "performance tours".

Pundits may resist the idea that "graf" can infiltrate design. But taggers like Ricky Plant possess a firm grasp of the spraycan's crossover charms. Plant says that graffiti forms embody modern flux and restlessness. "Graffiti is not so much drawing as gesture. Up on a wall it's big, it's bold, it's colourful. But the real test of tagging is to get those lines to flow and interlock. In that way, it's totally up-to-date and very influential."

Mark Jackson agrees; Plant's views, he says, are definitively strechno. "It's just like with computer software. You need to explore what's there, go with the style of that machine. Otherwise, you're not using the technology for its own sake. And you might as well be a typographer."

Jackson is a great believer, however, in mixing styles. "That's what I've learned from hip-hop and street graffiti and desktop publishing. You can stick anything together. And you can bootleg any style. That's what strechno is about - bootlegging imagery. It's just like hip-hop or modern lit, where you don't have to write your own stories any more. The basic stories are already there. You just take what you want, like the Dadaists did."

People are going to bootleg, says Jackson, because the images exist - and because it is now possible to produce or publish easily and cheaply. "But strechno art is ephemeral, too. That's a humbling thing to learn. Graffiti's great training because a piece only lasts as long as that specific style is in. When you hear kids talk about it they'll go, 'Yeah, it was great for 1986'. But it's 1990 now - so that no longer counts."

Jackson makes the point that "strechno is art for today. This is what you can do with the tomorrow of today. Reproduce it quickly, because these things only last as images."

Jackson's chosen metier - fanzines, flyers, legal graf - condemns his work to the underground. But, despite the fact he has also worked for Sunday colour supplements, for Vogue, City Limits, and Creative Review, fringe status is fine with him. "I worked for all those people as someone providing illustrations. But really, I was just ripping up ads and making the adverts I wanted to see. I've stayed underground and I'm happy with what I've done. Because once you become succesful, your art isn't really yours any more: you have to start serving clients. Their ideas of what they want to see are different from yours. And, at the end of the day, they're paying the bills. So you have to do what they want."

RAVE 2001

PRESENTS

WEST LONDON PRESSURE

AT
THE BRAIN.
11, WARDOUR STREET, W1
23rd APRIL.

AN EXHIBITION OF
WEST LONDON STREET STYLE.
SHOWING THE LATEST IN
SPRAY CAN AND XEROX ART.
FOLLOWED BY A THROWDOWN
FEATURING 3 OF WEST LONDON'S
FINEST D.J.'S:—

OUT OF MANY, WE ARE ONE

hot house and soul beats.

free-ness 8-4 11pm. £5 after.

BETWEEN the past AND THE FÜTÜRE

Change Yourself
for a
Positronic Future

Around the end of the 20th century, planet Earth, which had long
been acknowledged as one of the most backward planets in the
Universe, performed a quantum jump from medievilism into the
Positronic Future.

The elimination of power:
Positive human social development through a creative education.
A value of the universe through the perspective of co/operation

These aims and objectives determined the choice made by
millions of earth people for whom the Positronic Future opened
the doors to a new way of life.

The future that is projected is not an invention.
It is a positronic interpretation of how earth people complete the
Quantum jump, the transformation Between the past and the future.

The Technology is Now Available

You Can Not Stop
the Revolution

Jackson mixes music,
machines and spray-paint.
Examples here include, top
left: ticket for Rave 2001 at
the Wag Club; top right: two
pages from Jackson's
publication Positronic; left:
the West London Pressure
crew's business card (note:
telephone number no longer
correct); and right: a ticket
for London rappers the
Cash Crew

WEST LONDON PRESSURE

GRAFIK ARTISTS

TEL: 727-9601.

I'M GONNA CHECK THE
CASH CREW DOWN AT
THE TAB WITH D.J. ARG.
SAT. 14TH APRIL. £5 WITH
THIS TICKET BEFORE 11PM.
MORE AFTER!

TABERNACLE
POWIS SQUARE W11

Chris Long
Fashion Conscious Joe

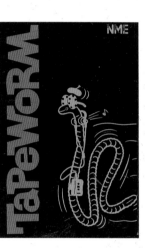

Long has continued to follow his funky muse through forms as well as across the Atlantic. Far left: a deck design for Slam City Skates. Left: a personal logo. Below, centre: cassette tape covers for New Musical Express. Bottom: illustration for the Sunday Times.

Chris Long is a visual translator. From the constantly shifting minutiae of street fashion, he chooses signal details and moments - then welds them into a vivid and stylised world which welcomes any viewer. His flyer art, skateboard designs and illustrations revel in sharp colours and bold strokes. But the assurance with which Long captures a fresh British beat is the product of an unusual odyssey.

It began in Blackpool, "Las Vegas on the Sea", where Long spent his adolescence and did his foundation studies at Blackpool College of Technology & Art. There, a pop environment (the "Golden Mile", the "pleasure beach"; the 60-foot tall plaster Gnome) provided a fitting parallel to Long's love of esoteric Americana - especially early '50s "mood music" by obscure names such as Perry Kingsley, Les Baxter, Bob Thompson, Martin Denny and Esquivel.

Like his youthful surroundings, these sounds were surreal but hardly subtle. They involved odd juxtapositions, like Hawaiian melodies, noisy birds, and Hollywood sound effects - a schtick which was echoed by sleeve art that featured scantily clad ladies, lunar landscapes, and titles such as "Other Worlds, Other Sounds" and "The In Sound From Way Out". "They weren't Easy Listening, either," says Long. "They come right out and hit you over the head. Ninety per cent of my records were and are black music, Northern soul. But I've always been fascinated by this sort of '50s aural madness."

In 1979, Long came to London to study at Hornsey School of Art (now Middlesex Polytechnic) and quickly established his regular hangouts: the Scala Cinema for American B-movies, and Dean Street for a weekly club night ("Dr D's Rhythm Miracle") he staged with flatmate Phil Sawyer. In both sites, his relationship with America's trash aesthetic flowered. "At college, I was making films, little super-8 things, like pop videos with a cartoon sexual subject. They had titles like 'The Black Magic Box' and 'New Religion'. Plus, at the club, we showed cartoons. We got some old Batman footage and re-edited that with Sawyer as Batman and me as

This sleeve for Phonogram Records "I Feel Better Than James Brown" by Was (Not) Was reflects Long's fascination with dressing-up and self-presentation, as well as the record-shop murals he had executed in America

Arriving home in 1988, Long landed in the middle of a new nightclub culture. He set out to capture its vitality in paintings like this one, for the LP "My Afro's On Fire" by Gee St Records' Outlaw Posse

Robin. The soundtrack was Northern soul records, plus early industrial stuff from Rough Trade."

In 1981, Long's girlfriend Sue (now his wife) got a job with an Italian couture house. Relocated to Rome, Long found work drawing strips for Frigidaire. He did them under pseudonyms, such as 'John O. London'. "Those jobs exposed me to the whole European cartoon scene: this glossy mag, with comic strips, and articles on the Mafia or necrophilia. A friend translated my strip, but the dialogue came out very broken, cracked Italian. I'd see people on the street burst out laughing as they read it."

Long's strips were sagas of British street chic ("Hip Joint"), or London life ("White Rastas", "Mr Joe") with bad Italian dialogue. "I realised then that was what I could do - I could translate London life. I could tell another culture something, purely through my eyes. So that's what I was going to be, a proper cartoon artist."

In the early 1980s, Long returned to England and met up with a kindred spirit - cartoonist Edwin Pouncey. As Savage Pencil, Pouncey had honed his art in the music press. He shared Long's love for junk music, B-culture, foreign cartoonery and black humour. And his roiling, apocalyptic

surrealism was the perfect match for Long's bold social portraiture. Until 1986, Pencil and Long worked as a team called "Battle of the Eyes" producing, among other items, their own underground comics - numbers with titles like "Nyak Nyak" and "Corpsemeat 2".

Meanwhile in 1984 Long had also started drawing for New Musical Express. He contributed regular comic strips, cover art and illustrations. "Eventually I became an Assistant Art Editor, working under Joe Ewart. But the paper was a lot of overgrown public schoolboys reminiscing about their nannies. And, when it came to cartoons, I still couldn't find a really good writer to work with." In 1987, Long and his wife left for California - a move which provided the turning-point in his art and gave him his own point of view.

"California was like a musical mecca for me, and I loved it," he says. "I got really into exotica; stuff like Esquivel which had fused the populist crazes of two cultures. Then we went to Mexico and that was a major influence. The vibrant colours and folk toys - the huge Diego Rivera murals and skeletons from the Day of the Dead. Those big, enclosed Mexican markets reminded me of Blackpool. There was no specific likeness, but

their feeling was the same. . . . Between California and Mexico I was somehow freed of my tie to Americana. It made me realise the British past was alive too: Dickensian stuff, even the Romans. I started to really look around me." Before he left San Francisco, however, Long executed his own mural - a lineup of UK music collectors, from soulboys to neo-mods - for a vintage record shop by the name of Roocky Riccardo's.

Long arrived home in '88, amidst London's explosion of club culture, hip-hop sound and sports-orientated fashion. "A social underground with a musical base and strong fashion connections - I loved it! It seemed like almost a metaphor for what had happened to me."

Long recognises that his method has matured. "I used to reach towards other cultures for a style. Now, it's like the pot has melted - and the things I draw are not an affectation, they're part of my own experience. Hip-hop and fashion, for instance, take a knowledge of the past and a less-than-parochial world for granted. They challenge people's knowledge of both. And, just like changes in fashion, that keeps you on your toes."

Half of Long's work is cartoon-strip crisp and music-press professional. The other half is composed of paintings like those above. Some end up as book covers or illustrations. Below, left: cover for Eyeball magazine; right: part of a running cartoon in New Musical Express. Centre: Long's portrait of his idol Esquivel; right: two tickets for EC1 Express club

Parker's individual slides can combine hand-
coloured xerography with photography and
computergraphics, as in this projection from
a programme commissioned for the 1987
National Jazz Awards. Above: his method is
also popular with art directors (here, an
illustration for a car-magazine article)

Allen F. Parker
Writing On The Walls

From the musical agitprop of rADical Wallpaper in
'79 through London Video Art's reels at High On
Hope ten years later, 3-D projection has always
played a part in clubs. But Allan F. Parker has
transformed the humble slide-show. Usually
featuring two carousels and 200 slides, Parker's
pieces are events in themselves. More than that,
they attempt to capture the actual climate of
modern leisure.

Parker sees that climate as increasingly global in
its aesthetics and concerns. "The first slide-show I
did as a musical collaboration was at the ICA in
1984. It was with a group called 'The Young
Pioneers', who were billed as 'from Dubrovnik'. Of
course, they were really from Camden - it was just
socialist chic." But ten years on, Britain is more
involved with the rest of the globe. Via the young
side of this new British worldliness, Parker's work
has travelled widely. He's worked on projects
destined for Tokyo, Kuala Lumpur, Singapore. But

Above left: credit sequence from a concert slide-show destined for the Far East. Above right: an image of nightlife from a slide-show commissioned by Wire magazine

Parker's original sponsorship came from club culture in the UK.

He generated ambience for musical events from the British Jazz Awards to the 1989 Time Out Live exhibit at Olympia. His slide-shows start with a single theme, then work to mutate it through real, as well as metaphorical, time. "The Cornflake Shop, for instance, commissioned a show for client parties, trade stands and private use. Their only brief was that it should also be connected with music. So the piece took off from the centre of a record. Which, during the course of the 'story', turned into a moon, then into various lights. The changes also involved four characters out on a journey through a fantasy cityscape." The finished work, Night Mail, resonates with the nocturnal romance of a modern metropolis. As with all Parker commissions, the clients receive a copy (in this case, comprised of 160 slides), but the designer retains copyright.

At first Parker constructed his slides by the simplest possible method: xerox copies and hand-tinting. "I would size up, copy, colour and manipulate my imagery, then collage it. Then I would photograph that from the screen of a video monitor." Over the years, he developed a range of ways to generate representations. "When I started out, there was always a deadline looming. Or else I had to work with other people's choice of material. All that was OK, but it wasn't where I wanted to stop."

In 1987, he linked up with Andy Golding, a staff teacher at the Polytechnic of Central London. Golding wanted to work with Parker, who welcomed his expertise. Together, they

approached PCL to let them use photographic and studio facilities. And now the college has access to everything they produce - for use as teaching tools.

And Parker can originate raw material himself. It varies from a "meteor shower" (rocks painted with fluorescent tones, then photographed against black velvet with a zoom lens) to the trampolinist in air who will make up the slide's other half. We do that with front-projection," he says. "Which is great because you can shoot the backgrounds anywhere - or make them up through collage, computergraphics, whatever." The trampoline artist helps him to escape the limits of gravity: "Otherwise, everything happens at the bottom of your frame." But it took seven people and £500 to do the trampoline shoot - and that's not counting the meteorites or making all the sandwiches. When you want people to work for free, you have to make bloody good food!"

When a show projects, stills like the meteor shower and flying girl will be superimposed; slowly those superimpositions will dissolve into others. "To combine your figures," says Parker, "you work out where all the spaces will be, and how they'll intersect. But to represent it on paper - to send proposals abroad, for instance - you have to dupe them together." Usually, he sends prospective clients a sample show and a set of colour xeroxes.

He has created slide-shows to every kind of music: bhangra, rap, jazz. But Parker's work encapsulates particularly the juxtaposition, homage and humour of dancefloor sound. "That's exactly what we do," he says. "We sample, select

and re-mix. I've seen my things loads of times in other people's work; I see them going by all the time in pop videos. And it's a fair cop. That's the nature of sampling."

In the mid-'80s, Parker produced and published his own series of 28 postcards. These were sold in Switzerland, Japan and Australia as well as around the UK. But he prefers teaching to full-time commercial and editorial work. "It does look great, especially for musical projects. But it's also quite complicated to do stuff like this for sleeve art. And it gets a lot more expensive. To copy onto 2.25, you've got to have a bellows. And all your source material must be on 2.25 as well."

In contrast, the 35mm slide allows Parker room for experiment and spontaneity. "What I do is simple. But it's very labour-intensive. And you've got to know what images are going to work together." He points to a single slide: "Riding in this car are Madonna, Ray Charles, the Empire State Building, a 1930s Canadian tourist and Tina Weymouth on guitar!"

The biggest shows Parker and Golding have done were a series called The Psychic Ball, commissioned by Japan's Fujipacific, and staged in two Tokyo nightclubs. But they are now developing a Bombay stadium show for Boy George. Parker admits that, despite work like that of Housewatch and rADical Wallpaper, slide-shows are perceived as a totally fringe pursuit. "For a long time, I was trying to make it more like 'art' - because that's what I trained for. Now, I've come to realise I can do more of what I want. Besides, I'm still developing it. So I'll keep on going."

Above: cover for a
Christmas issue
which combines
the array of
featured pieces
with an air of
festivity. Top left:
image from a retail
slide-show; below
left: illustration
commissioned by
the Sunday Times.
Below: Parker's
slides are
designed to
operate in
sequence, with at
least two
projected into one
place

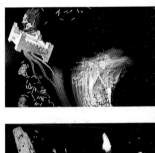

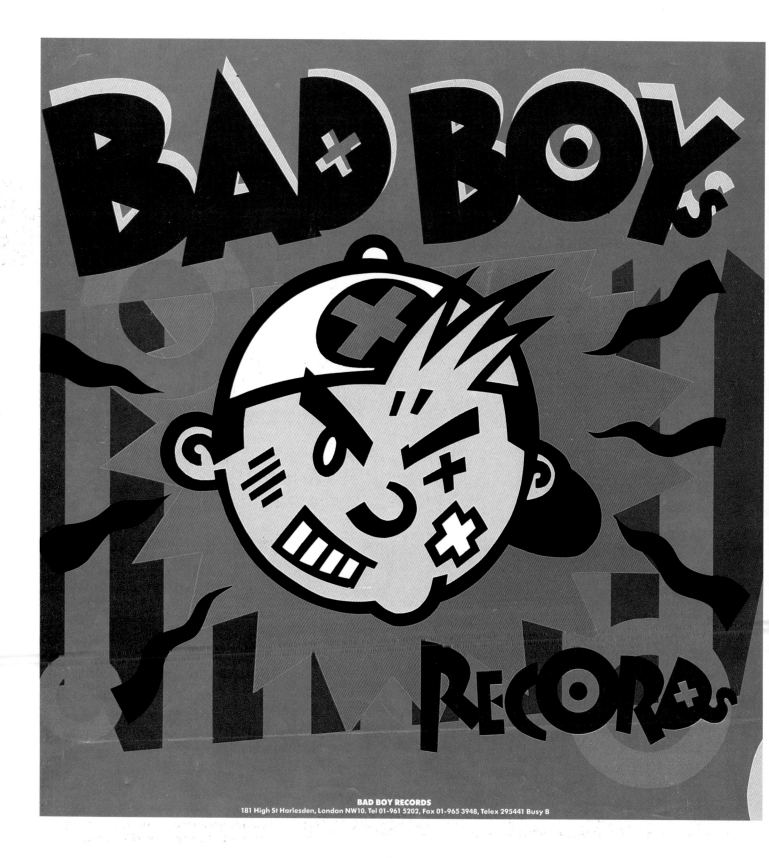

BAD BOY RECORDS
181 High St Harlesden, London NW10. Tel 01-961 5202, Fax 01-965 3948, Telex 295441 Busy B

136

Companies sought Jackson's skill at conveying the essence of an emerging musical style, such as house music or hip-hop. Opposite page: a "house bag" or promotional sleeve for Bad Boy Records. Right: sleeve for "Shocking Blue", a 12" by Champion Records' act Venus. Centre: club tickets, left, for EC1 Express (drawings: Chris Long), and Jackson's logo for his studio, Bite It! Bottom: 7" singles bag for Bass Records

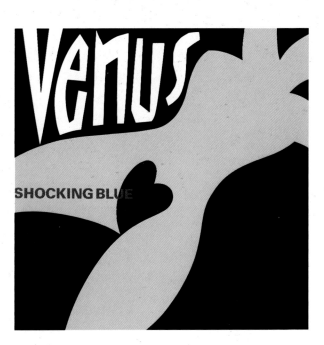

SHOCKING BLUE

"It's hard for ordinary people to appreciate graphic design as such," says Trevor Jackson. "They don't leaf through a record bin going, 'Ooh, that's a nice bit of Helvetica Light.' But I try to work for the average punter. I aim for the Debbies and Sharons who pick up a record to say, 'Wow! That's a great cover!'"

Trevor Jackson runs his own, one-man design firm: Bite It! The name comes from the hip-hop universe, where to "bite" a sound or piece of graffiti means to lift or appropriate it for one's own work. "It's not meant to be subtle," says Jackson. "The idea was, 'This is good, so bite this, mate!'"

A DJ at clubs like Megabite, Jackson craves the challenge of translating London's pulsating nightlife into graphic terms. He found his first outlet with a tiny musical independent, Champion Records. "Because I had so little money," he says, "I tried to be very simple at first. I developed strong, iconic logos with extra touches like spot varnish - in order to give things a little depth."

Via Champion's quick turnover of acts, Jackson honed those logos into something he calls pictograms. "They're symbols, where illustration and design can come together. I'm interested in direct images which exploit the energy of opposites - positive and negative; male and female. The part of design that's to do with controlling your thoughts and getting them down in two dimensions."

In late 1988, Jackson executed album sleeves, cassette covers, 12" single sleeves and T-shirts for New York rappers the Jungle Brothers - work which won him the attention of other designers as well as major labels like WEA and MCA Records. But even with more work than he can handle, Jackson relies on primary powers when it comes to his designs. "More than anything else, I get inspired by the actual records. But it's very very important to be flexible. Half of this business is

An affinity for strong, iconic imagery permeates Jackson's work. Above, from left: logo for Chrysalis Records' dance label Cooltempo Records; logo for a coalition of Warner Brothers Records' rappers; Bite It!'s 1991 logo; logo for militant London Jewish rap trio The Brotherhood. Bottom: Champion Records 7" singles bags for Liquid Oxygen, left, and Raze, right

meeting people and being able to listen to what they say. You've got to meet the band, understand who commissions you."

Not that he always takes the advice of musicians' company representatives. "Mostly, I work for people who want something they know is me. But I have to give 'em a lot of blag. Like the first time I went into Chrysalis. They said, 'Now, for this initial single, we want something which will establish the band.' And I said 'No you don't - you want something that's gonna blow people's heads!'"

Jackson's social orbit is not composed of other designers. "Talking about design is just incredibly boring; I don't really mix with designers at all. I'd rather talk about music and fashion and life. I'm into haircuts, Saul Bass typography, JD King cartoons. I'm just trying to make things fun."

The Jacksonian analysis of fun, however, is not simplistic. This designer is an anti-elitist, a social subversive who thinks every citizen needs to think for himself. "You can't not look at other work, otherwise you get ignorant," he says. "But I don't

see it as competition. I just want to stretch myself. The best design coming out now is exactly like the best music; it's made by people without faces or massive egos. Don't get me wrong. Of course I'd like a bit of fame. But I prefer the underground vibe. Like around my studio, where they're knocking down all the old buildings, there's some guy stickin' up these great little posters saying 'Death By Demolition'. It's like a pirate flag, a skull with two little cranes behind it. And that's what I call design - 'cause it lets you fight with your mind."

All he does, says Jackson, is apply "proper design" principles. But when it comes to music, he claims, graphics are still the poor relation. "Generally, I think there's far too much emphasis placed on photography. It should be 'Sod all that! Ideas are the most important thing!' It's crap when the idea's bad and someone says, 'Oh, just jazz it up with some happenin' i-D graphics'."

He would never give up his record sleeves. ("At school I didn't get technical teaching as such; those

are my learning ground.") But Jackson would like to move his design into other dimensions. "I'd love to do magazine work, I'd love to do clothes. I'd like to design a magazine. I'd like to do a club and do the tickets and banners and clothing - do the whole lot. I'd also like to do film titles.

"But I don't want to form a big company and have some Renaissance set-up where other people begin to design and I still take the credit. I'm happy. To be quite honest, I'd be happy to work for myself with maybe one assistant for the rest of my natural life." Communal endeavour, however, does play a part in Jackson's working life. For instance, he's an unofficial member of the team known as "UTO": stylists Derrick Procope and Karl Templer's Unlimited Talent Organisation. For UTO, the designer does graphics, trades information and gossip - even does the occasional unofficial modelling.

"Basically," says Jackson, "my desires are simple. I just want to buy all the records I want and keep going out every night."

As a tyro designer, Jackson depended on smaller, independent labels to serve as laboratories for the development of his style. For such employers, he could work in many formats. Above, a 7" house bag, or DJ promo sleeve, for Champion Records

GEE STREET

5 017640 200146

NEW
Portable 12" Single

STEREO   ⦿

GEE T14

BASS

A SIDE

FUNTOPIA

Friendly Technology

featuring JIMMI POLO

FREEDOM

Feel the Beat

G

LIBERATION MIX

A FUNTOPIA PRODUCTIO

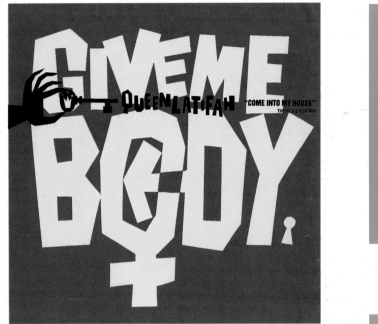

The explosion of 12" remixes by famous producers, celebrity DJs and personalities gave designers a fresh challenge. Opposite page: a 12" remix of "Freedom" by Funtopia, featuring Jimmi Polo. Top: the Richie Rich mix of Queen Latifah's "Come Into My House" on Gee St Records; right: Champion's 12" "Dance", from Earth People; Below: a double A-side sleeve, by Champion Records artists Lee Marrow

GEESTREET

PM DAWN
(Prince B + Minute Mix Master)

"ODE TO A FORGETFULL MIND"
ULTIMATUM MIX

GEET 24

5 017640 200245

ZULU

His work for the Jungle Brothers brought Jackson to the attention of the industry. Above: a drawing for their single "Black Is Back". Left: Gee St Records' sticker publicising a new mix

YOU'LL NEVER GET TO HEAVEN
F JOEY'S GROOVE

Leta Davis
YOU'LL NEVER GET TO Heaven

Left: a 7" sleeve for Lita Davis' remake of Burt Bacharach's "You'll Never Get To Heaven", on Champion Records.

SP

WARNING!

Bite it! Recordings

Above, left to right: logo for Eric B and Rakim's "The Microphone Fiend"; logo for Secret Promotions; Warning! sticker for a De La Soul LP (indicating it was unavailable in America); logo for Jackson's own label

Hip-Hop, with its self-promotional orbit of ever-changing fashion, attitudes and issues, fascinates Jackson, and he loves trying to capture it on the sleeves he undertakes. Above: sleeve for "33 45 78", debut album by London rap group the Stereo MCs

Funky graphics, says the designer, are something which he assimilates from toys, magazines, and television graphics
from the 1950s and '60s. Above: a 12" sleeve for Champion Records' Aphrodisiac's "Song of the Siren"

hrough Trevor Jackson, the Champion
Records label has managed to acquire a
trong, smart visual identity which can only
enefit the label's acts. Right: singles bag for
ony Scott's "Gangster Boogie", Champion;
entre, left to right: logos to be used in-house
r an Information Sheet, Artist Biographies,
romotion and Newsheet. Bottom: another
ingles bag, "Reach Up to Mars", for
hampion's Earth People

Derek Yates
Myth Construed

Before he even reached university, designer Derek Yates saw his T-shirt designs bootlegged around the world. As the artist who put a face to North London's Soul II Soul, Yates's work is now part of black music's collective visual consciousness. And Soul II Soul's recording success has made his image, the "Funki Dred", a mainstream media icon.

It began with pirate broadcasting in 1985. "I did a T-shirt design for Contrast Radio," Yates tells it, "and Jazzie B saw that. Then a friend of mine did a club with Jazzie, a thing called 'Portland's '80s' in Euston. I did the flyers for it. And I told 'em they should change the name - to something like Serious Shit." They did. And, from then on, Jazzie B and his partner Philip "Daddae" Harvey have come to Derek for promo art. In March 1986, Yates designed the original Soul II Soul T-shirt - the enigmatic face now known as "the Funki Dred head".

"At that time," he remembers, "a lot of white clubbers were into wearing these little, round dark glasses. So I envisioned amalgamating the roughneck reggae lot with them. Because clubs were bringing those people together. And I wanted a symbol of that." His iconographic Funki Dred is also a portrait - of Soul II Soul's "roots man" and system expert Daddae Harvey.

Two months after designing the T-shirt, Yates left for four months' travel in Israel and the Middle East. "Travel is very important, I'm a great believer in it. If more people travelled, there'd be far less nationalism. The world would improve a lot." When Yates returned to London, he found Soul II Soul's big warehouse parties had made them neighbourhood stars. So he did some more designs for the crew - including a Soul II Soul comic strip. Then, in October '86, he left for Sussex University, to study Social Administration.

There Yates soon found himself designing T-shirts for the university. "At first I started just to make money. Then I thought, I'm doing this stuff all the time - why don't I give in and study art?" By 1987, he was enrolled in a foundation course at Camberwell School of Arts and Crafts. And since 1988 he has

With inspirations that range from aboriginal art to the vibrant religious imagery he seeks out on his travels, Yates attempts to import freshness and optimism into the UK. For him, it is a symbol of dancefloor art and camaraderie. Left: a design for the Nightclubbing page of Echoes magazine

Whether they come from faery tales or Rastafarian beliefs, visual mythologies fascinate Yates, who aims to create new ones as he pursues sequences of designs. Above: one of several computer-generated 1991 logos for Soul II Soul. Right: selection from a series of linocuts

Left: for London boutique Confusion, Yates developed a range of designs for different purposes: club tickets, shop cards and T-shirts. Below centre: a separate T-shirt design on the theme of Ecology

been at Brighton Poly. All the time, he has stayed in touch with Jazzie and Soul II Soul. And when their retail outlets opened, Yates - along with the collective's other designers - began to supply more wearable art. It had a knock-on effect among other designers and club promoters. Soon they were ringing him up for everything from sportswear to flyers.

Yates avoids most such work to concentrate on his course. But his basic aesthetic adheres to the qualities which first attracted Jazzie B. He aims for vivid, bold designs, which marry the strength and spiritual poise of "primitive" art to the Britain of today. "My first serious paintings were to do with aborigines and the nature of their visual culture. Which was because I had read this book called Songlines, by Bruce Chatwin. But the more I saw of other so-called primitive arts, the more I was moved by their beauty and their assurance."

Mythologies have always intrigued him. "I now realise I'd really like to create a fresh visual myth. Something really relevant to London in the '90s. So I've been coming up with these big, bright linocuts. Satires that dress these weird Greek figures in giant trainers and heavy chains."

Confidence is a Yates trait. Yet self-assurance in one so young has rarely been smiled on at college: "One guy at college always tells me, 'You've got to learn to sing the quiet tunes.' But I'm not really into that. Subtlety is not my thing." Some of his projects have also taken Yates's tutors by surprise. His woodcuts of "Little Red Riding Hood", for instance, end with Red making love to the wolf. ("I envisioned her as the product of a rigid Catholic background," Yates says, smiling.)

Yates's work resonates with the energy of a multi-racial generation who know their time has come. And Soul II Soul, he says, provided a perfect training-ground for him. "A lot of my earliest stuff would be considered weak by professional design standards. But it taught me something very important: why you pay attention to what people like. I really do believe that art should please the people who see it. More often than not, designers today just ignore that."

He says that he's "into mythologies and art from other cultures, partly because they are understood by ordinary people in the street." And he tries to investigate such inspirations on site. In May 1990, for instance, he travelled to Rumania - in order to

design and paint murals inside orphanages there. He then spent the following summer traversing most of India. "In that culture, everyone of every class is an artist. The shrines, the charms, the graffiti - it's brilliant. The country is just completely decorated. Even down to the patterns of rice they pour on the ground outside each door."

Yates won't finish college until mid-1991. But as he begins those final terms, he's also back at work for Soul II Soul; and there are other shops, flyers and T-shirt designs. All in training, he maintains, for the studio he hopes to found. True to sound system theory, this will be a centre whose team of designers oversee - and control - their every product. "So you get your T-shirt out on the street when its graphics are really fresh. You make sure it's printed just as you want. And no one crops or distorts your designs. Because you handle the type, the colours, the run - the lot - in-house."

He considers this really important "because in Britain retail is now controlled by a few big corporations. They pick up on things young artists do, clean off the edges and make 'em 'sophisticated'. Then they sit back and collect the money. And where does that leave you?"

Another sample sleeve for Soul II Soul (linocut), which utilises the circle-of-friends motif as well as ideas like street fashion and dramatic self-presentation, which Yates would eventually pursue in a painting for the 12" sleeve of Soul II Soul's "Get A Life"

For Soul II Soul and various clubs where that collective's members have worked as DJs, Yates has served as a house artist. Opposite page: the original Funki Dred head, a portrait of Phillip "Daddae" Harvey in which Yates tried to marry Harvey's ragga style to white London street chic. The combination proved a portent of events and sounds to come. Above: one of a series of early sleeve designs for Jazzie B

Above: sleeve design for Bang The Party's "Back to Prison"; right: in the Yates vision of contemporary London as mythic, heroes wear trainers and consciousness badges, as well as Rasta hats

151

Additional
Information

Artists' Curricula Vitae

TREVOR JACKSON
1983-87 West Barnet College,
Diploma in General Art & Design
Higher National Diploma, Graphic Design
Exhibitions: 1989 Creative Futures, London,
Hamiltons Gallery
Clients: Champion Records, WEA Records,
MCA Records, Gee Street Records, Island
Records, Chrysalis Records

Bite It!
74 Clerkenwell Rd
London EC1M 5QA
071-608-2517

IAN SWIFT
1981-83 Foundation Course, Warrington Art
College
1983-86 Manchester Polytechnic, BA Hons
Graphic Design
1986-88 Designer, The Face
1988-89 Designer, Arena
1988-90 Designer, Neville Brody Studio
1990 -91 Art Director, Arena Magazine
Present: Art Director, Straight No Chaser;
Creative Director, Talking Loud Records
(Phonogram). Other clients: Meets Regional
Magazine (Tokyo); Paul Smith; Toni & Guy
Hairdressing; Super Mirage Topwave (Tokyo);
SBK Records, CBS Records, Font Shop, Island
Records,Thames and Hudson.
Exhibitions:1986 The Different Kitchen:
Commercial Art in Manchester, 1976-86
1990 Creative Direction Showcase, Smith's
Galleries, London

43B Coronet St
London N1 6HD
071-613 1759
Fax: 071-613-1703

THE THUNDERJOCKEYS
Graham Elliott
1980-83 Manchester Polytechnic BA Hons
Graphic Design
1985-87 Royal College of Art, MA Hons
Illustration
John England
1980-83 Kingston Polytechnic, BA Hons
1983-86 Royal College of Art, MA Hons
Illustration
Working as The Thunderjockeys since May
1986
1989-January 1990 Saatchi & Saatchi
Presently: BMP DDB Needham
Performances: 1987 'Spectacle Yummy
Yummy'; Zeebelt Theatre, Den Haag, Holland

'Desire'; F.I.T., New York
1986 'Time Waltz'; Royal College of Art
Awards: D&AD Silver Award, 1990 (for design
of European Illustration 1989-1990)
Magazine design: 1990: Videographic
Clients: Swatch; Studio Dunbar, Holland; CBS
Records America; CBS Records UK; MTV
Europe; MTV America; British Satellite
Broadcasting; Royal College of Art; Marlboro
Music Munich; Thompson Publishing;
European Illustration; Sky magazine; A la Carte
magazine; Interview magazine; 19 magazine;
Creative Review; Young & Rubicam; Doyle,
Dane, Bernbach; Lowe Howard Spink;
WCRSMM: DMB&B; Penguin; Bloomsbury;
Heinemann; Jonathan Cape; Wolf Olins;
Ziggaratt; Michael Peters; David Davies; A&M
Records; Chrysalis Records; Serious Music;
RCA Records; MCA Records; Virgin Records;
Sleeping Bag Records; Virgin Records; WEA
Records

John England
Tomato
26-27 D'Arblay St
London W1B 3FH
071-434-0955
Fax: 071-434-0935

Graham Elliott
155 East 49th St (Apt 2F)
New York, NY 10017 USA
212-753-8226

PAUL ELLIMAN
1980-82 Portsmouth Polytechnic
1986-88 Design Director, Wire magazine
1988 Panellist, Design & Art Direction Awards
(Editorial & Book Design)
Clients: City Sports (US), Wire, City Limits,
Verso, Meets Regional (Japan), Cornflake
Shop, Leading Edge UK, IB Taurus, The
Photographer's Gallery, Brixton Village Arts
Centre, The Holborn Centre For the Performing
Arts, The Unknown, Artist (West Germany),
Kunst (West Germany)

47 Lion Mills
392-396 Hackney Rd
London E2 7AP
071-623-0378

MARK JACKSON
1977-81 Stockport College of Technology,
Graphic & Advertising Design Diploma
1986-88 Proprietor of own sign-writing
company

1989-90 West London Pressure, working from
Tabernacle Community Centre
Exhibitions: 1987/1988 "From Metal To
Canvas", London, Tabernacle Community
Centre
1988 "Too Damn Tough", London, Tabernacle
Community Centre
1989 "Untold Stories, Unseen Realms",
London, Southwark Art Gallery
1989 "West London Pressure", London, Grove
Cafe
1990 "West London Pressure", London, The
Brain Club
1990 "The Fabulous Sprayers", Milan
Clients: The Fred, International Herald Tribune,
New Statesman, City Limits, Creative Review,
Whistles, The Independent, The Observer, BBC
Breakfast TV, Stanter Alta Nova (Milan), 01-For
London, BBC World Service, Creative Review,
Vogue, Association of Youth Clubs, Soul II Soul,
Virgin Records
Fax: 081-968-3660

IAN WRIGHT
1974-75 Goldsmiths College of Art
1975-78 London College of Printing
Exhibitions: 1979 "Artificial Light", Newcastle
Polytechnic
"Shoes", London, Neal Street Gallery
1980 "Heads or Tails", Newcastle Polytechnic
"Flowers & Animals", London, Neal Street
Gallery
1983 "Pieces of Art", London, Association of
Illustrators Gallery
1983 Association of Illustrators Annual
Exhibitions
1985 "Wild Crayons", Centre d'Exposition
Canrobert, Jouy-en-Josas, France
Clients: A&M Records; Blast Magazine; City
Limits magazine; Creative Diary; EMI Records;
The Face magazine; Arena magazine; Lewis
Moberley; New Musical Express; Performance
Car magazine; Rolling Stone; Sunday Times
magazine; Playboy Jazz Festival; Polydor
Records; Virgin Records; Classical Music
magazine; WEA Records; Phonogram Records;
Straight No Chaser magazine; CBS Records;
Goethe Institute; Zarjazz Records; The Wire
magazine; LA Style magazine; Playboy
magazine; London Weekend Television; TWBA

In UK: Unit 2
Whitehorse Yard
78 Liverpool Rd
London N1
081-881-3431
In Japan: Junko Wong

Cross World Connections
Stork Daikanyama #402
2-26-15 Higashi
Shibuya-ku, Tokyo 150, Japan
03-5466-0715
Fax: 03-5466-0716

GEORGE GEORGIOU

1978-79 Hornsey College of Art, Foundation (Art & Design)
1979-82 Leicester Polytechnic, BA Hons 3D Design
1989-present: Runs own company, General Practice
1987-89 Godsmark Gordon; Partner
1985-87 Hop Studio; Senior Designer
1983-85 Carmona Dover; Junior Designer
1982-83 John S Bonnington Partnership; Junior Designer
Clients: Courage, Ltd; TSB Building Societies; Terry Gilliam (domestic design); Sea Containers; Pied A Terre; Ted Bates; Salisbury House; Food Street (Trocadero); Singapore Sam; Dover, Sweeney & Partners; Born To Shop; AXIA Architects; ABC (children's shop); Starship Enterprises; Wicked Management; Habit; Time Out magazine; Creative Review; i-D magazine; The Face magazine; MTV Europe
Club clients: BB Crop; RAW; Do At the Zoo; Shoom; Sin; City of Angels; Alphabet City; Special Branch; Last Temptation; Milk Bar

Basement Flat
25 Lanhill Rd
London W9 2BS
071-289-4651

FIONA HAWTHORNE

1982-83 Belfast Art College
1983-86 Chelsea School of Art, BA Hons Design/Illustration
1989 Sir John Cass School of Art, Postgraduate Printmaking
Exhibitions: 1987 Belfast Christmas Show (group show), Fenderesky Gallery, Belfast London Competition; London Institute Exhibitions, Royal Festival Hall
1988 'Alive & Kicking', Jazz Cafe
1989 'Public Faces, Private Views', Tricycle Theatre
'Artists and Audience', London, Harolds Gallery
'Drawings of Theatre & Music', London, Soho Poly Theatre
1990 Crawley Jazz Festival
Clients: Institute of Contemporary Art, Soho Poly Theatre, Gate Theatre, Watermans' Art

Centre, Royal Court Theatre, Next Directory, Lamb & Shirley, Harrods, Tatler magazine, Harpers & Queen magazine, Wire magazine, Pandora Books, Rhythm King Records, Island Records, Stylus Records, Channel 4 (Big World Cafe, Club X, Jazz Classics), Spellbound Pictures, MTV, Final Vinyl Records, Castle Hendring

47 Barlby Rd
London W10
081-968-8889

DEREK YATES

1986-87 University of Sussex
1987-88 Camberwell College of Arts & Crafts
1988-present Brighton Polytechnic
Clients: Sussex University, Contrast Radio, Confusion (club and shop), Unity Sportswear, Warriors Dance, Soul II Soul, AVL Records

081-808-3287

CHRIS LONG

1976-78 Blackpool College of Technology & Art, Foundation
1978-81 Middlesex Polytechnic, BA Hons, Fine Art

1982-83: Lived & worked in Rome; regular cartoons included: "Mr Joe"; "The Hip Joint"; "Crazy Dreams"; "White Rastas"
1983-87; Freelance illustration & T-shirt design; Assistant Art Editor, New Musical Express; strip artist, Escape magazine; regular cartoons included "Wide Boys"; "Trogga"; "Other People"; "This Is London"
1984-85: Formed "Battle of the Eyes" partnership with Savage Pencil (Edwin Pouncey); published Nyack-Nyack (with Andy Dog) & Corpsemeat 2
1987-88 Lived & worked in San Francisco: cartoonist; muralist
1988-present: Freelance illustration, design, cartoons
Exhibitions: 1989 "Eurovisioni"; Milan
Films: "Kookie, Kookie, Lend Me Your Comb"; "New Religion"; "The Black Magic Box" (The Early Broadcast Company)
Clients: Escape magazine; Frigidaire (Italy); Gee Street Records; Arena magazine; Office of Fair Trading; New Musical Express; Slam City Skates; Radio One; Rough Trade Records; Sunday Times magazine; Picabia (Japan); Marks & Spencer

In UK: The Inkshed
98 Columbia Rd
London E2 7QB
071-613-2323
Fax: 071-613-2726

In Japan: Junko Wong
Cross World Connections
Stork Daikanyama #402
2-26-15 Higashi
Shibuya-ku, Tokyo 150, Japan
03-5466-0715
Fax: 03-5466-0716

ALLAN FORRESTER PARKER

1974-78 Reading University, BA Hons (1st Class) Fine Art
1983-84 Hertfordshire College of Art, Postgraduate Diploma in Art & Psychology
Exhibitions & Shows:
1979 Arnolfini Gallery, Bristol: Performance, sculpture, photography
1980-81 Three Projects; London ICA
1982 Slade School of Art: Performance piece
1984 Young Pioneers, London ICA (slide-show)
1987 Night-Town, 1987 British Jazz Awards (slide-show)
1988 Night Mail, commissioned by The Cornflake Shop for Time Out Live 1988 (slide-show)
The Sushi Show, commissioned by Simon Browne; Cobden Working Men's Institute (slide-show)
1989 The Psychic Ball, commissioned by Fujipacific and Salonmusic (slide-shows); Club Quatro, Shibuya, Tokyo
Other clients: National Student; Sunday Times magazine; Wire magazine; Performance Car magazine; Microdecision; Director magazine; The Mail On Sunday; Marie-Claire magazine; The Face magazine; Creative Review; The Observer magazine; SKY magazine; Penguin Books; Quartet Books; Brannan; Rogers & Rippington; Redwood Publishing; Young & Rubicam; The Original Propshop; Channel 4.
Teaching: Since 1988, Video Projects for The Polytechnic of Central London; 1984, Working Men's College, taught Yang Style T'ai Chi; 1989, Working Men's College, began to teach Chen style T'ai Chi

58 Whidbourne Buildings
London WC1H 8HG
Phone/FAX: 071-278-4507

Additional Contact Information

Design After Dark deals with the London dancefloor only. But the following contacts may be of use to readers:

Anarchic Adjustment Clothing Designs
In UK: see Slam City Skates
In US: 1250 Suite E Yard Court
San Jose
California 95133
(area code 408) 292-5962
British skater-designer Nick Phillips' clothing designs range from sportswear and hats to T-shirt prints and jackets. In the UK, they are licensed through London's Slam City Skates.

Black Market Records
25 D'Arblay St
London W1
071-437-0478
Upfront, garage, acid and house music. Sells T-shirts, concert tickets (cash-only for the latter). Hours: Mon-Wed, Fri: 10am-7pm; Thurs: 10am-9pm; Sat: 10am-8pm; Sun:1pm-6pm.

Big, Broad & Massive Promotions
Hackney Youth In Progress
380 Old Street
London EC1V 9LS
071-739-8549
Retails tapes, videos, T-shirts, stickers and posters, including Clive Woodstock's pop and raggamuffin caricatures (Mike Tyson, Nigel Benn, the "New Scotland Yardie", etc). Holds street stalls all week in Ridley Rd Market, Hackney; every Saturday at Bradbury St Market, Hackney and Sunday at Petticoat Lane Market, Aldgate as well as Camden Lock Market, Camden Town every Saturday and Sunday. Also mail order catalogue.

Blame, Judy
Fax: 071-289-4487
London's premier guerilla stylist (has created images and clothing for stars who range from Neneh Cherry to Kylie Minogue) is as at home in the pages of Vogue as he is at pop video shoots. Also a well-known jewellery designer.

Copyart Photocopying Resource Centre
Culross Buildings, Battle Bridge Rd, Kings Cross, London NW1; 071-833-4417.
Layout & pasteup training, £6 per hour; design training, £10 per hour. Will also do "drop-off" copying. Maintain an "image bank" and a design service as well as computers and word-processing equipment. For details and to book time on a machine, telephone. Opening times: Mon-Fri (except Tues) 10am-6pm, Sat 11am-5pm. Hourly rate for copying: 50p concessions and £1 waged; workshops: £15 per hour but negotiable.

Creative Hands
Unit F
7 Willow St
London EC2 4AH
071-729-2635
Design studio founded and run by young black Britons to handle graphic, video and product design; fashion promotions and much more.

Groove Records
52 Greek St
London W1
071-439-8231
Started 16 years ago by Jean Palmer, Groove has heard dancefloor trends come and go, from electro to rap. Specialty is getting import hip-hop sounds in quick. When closed, shutters offer a lively display of UK graffiti art. Hours: Mon-Sat: 10am-7pm; Sun:2pm-6pm.

GWBB
42 Lancaster Gate
(N/E corner of square, basement)
London W2
071-723-5190
071-723-1583
Quick range of cost-effective video services including transfer of British and American tapes, tape copying, etc. Ring or drop in for full information.

Honest Jon's Records
278 Portobello Rd
London W10 5TE
081-989-9822
Fax: 081-969-4724
Two-floor vinyl paradise of soul, funk, fusion, rare grooves and hip-hop, incorporating a specialist Jazz Basement and the Reggae Revive shop (original UK and Jamaican 7", 12" LPs and re-issues: 1962-1979; hours noon-6pm, Thurs, Fri and Sat). Also worldwide mail-order service with separate catalogues covering Jazz on CD and eclectic acid-jazz. For catalogue, send large sae. Honest Jon's hours: Mon-Sat: 10am-6pm;Sun 11am-5pm.

Insane Casuals
In UK: Slam City Skates (see below)
In Japan: Mr Kojima
Made in World
2F Maruei Building
1-9-7 Jinnan
Shibuya-ku, Tokyo, Japan
Fax: 01081-33770-6579
Range of T-shirts, sport and casualwear by skater-artist Ged Wells and designer Sofia Prantera; available by mail order via Slam City. The catalogue itself is a work of graphic art, as Wells also creates Insane videos, toys and cartoons.

Kiss-FM shop
Kiss House
80 Holloway Rd
London N7 8JG
071-700-6100

T-shirts, hats, leggings, bumper stickers and other promo goods advertising the onetime pirate, now-legit radio station. Hours: Saturday only: 10am-6pm.

London Cartoon Centre
14 Conlan St
London W10 5AR
081-969-4562
This centre offers daytime training courses in cartoon skills: drawing, strip construction, composition, lettering, etc. Guest instructors have included some top names. Applicants must be aged between 16 and 25, available in the daytime, and living within reach of W10 area. A £30 deposit is required but is refunded on completion of the course. Ask for Eve Stickler.

London Film-Makers' Co-op
42 Gloucester Ave
London NW1 8JD
Workshop enquiries: 081-722-1728
Admin & distribution: 081-586-4806
Able to put would-be club promoters in touch with several groups and individuals specialising in portable visuals. Main purpose is to stockpile independent film; also runs own cinema of same.

Poizone Skate Designs
c/o Clan Skates
45 Hyndland St
Partick
Glasgow G11 8QF
041-339-6523
Skater-designers Jamie Blair and Davey Phillips design their range of sportswear with a Gaelic consciousness. The shop which stocks them is also their own.

Reckless Records
30 Berwick St
London W1
071-437-4271
Secondhand vinyl mecca for rare grooves, oddball obsessions, recently ditched review copies. The spot where Jonathon More and

Matt Black of Coldcut fame met. Hours: 10am-7pm every day.

The Rub
Unit 11
Portobello Green Arcade
281 Portobello Rd (under flyover)
London W10
081-964-1662
Fax: 081-968-3660
Exuberantly streetwise design consultancy: offers contract T-shirt printing and design; flyer and poster design, bannerworks, backdrops, graffiti-to-order, typography, textiles and more by talented ex-graffiti artist Ricky Plante, and associates Peter Corry and William Timother.

Scott Duncan PR
Unit 222, Canalot Production Studios
22 Kensal Rd
London W10
081-964-1144
Fax: 081-964-4262
The press team which helped shape Soul II Soul handles a wide range of clients, from fashion and hip-hop to mainstream music and film, actors and individual projects. Sandra Scott and Sandie Duncan specialise in representing young black artists, from Europe and America as well as within England.

Sketchy Magazine Skateboard Clothing
Box 37
146 Eglinton Rd
Plumstead
London SE18 3SY
As seen in Paul Browne's caricature-skatezine Sketchy. *Shirts, Sweatshirts, and back issues of* Sketchy *and* Sketchy Division; *stickers. Write for further information.*

Slam City Skates
16 Neals Yard
London WC2
Slam City : 071-240-0928;071-221-7495
Rough Trade 071- 240-0105

Fax: 071-221-1146
Skate shop upstairs from an unmatched array of indie, hardcore and nouveau punk records, T-shirts, artists' books, indie concert tickets, fanzines and so on. Retails T-shirts, decks, wheels, shoes, stickers, skatemags and similar including Poizone, Insane, Anarchic Adjustment and other British designer labels, as well as Mambo, Stussy, Life's A Beach and mainstream fashions. Hours: Mon-Sat, 10 am-6:30 pm.

Soul II Soul
36-38 Rochester Place
London NW1 9JX
071-284-0393
Fax: 071-284-0166
Soul II Soul's own line of designer sports and casual wear; retail by appointment; mail order by catalogue (send sae).

Unlimited Talent Organisation
Karl Templar (081-989-0961)
Derrick Procopé (081-969-0569)
or at *The Face*
071-837-7270
Fax: 071-837-3906
Templar and Procopé's organisation is primarily a set of fashion stylists. But like all good sound-system collectives, they can supply image/advice for many other kinds of affair: theatrical events, fashion shoots, pop videos, promotional photos, etc. Contact them as above or at The Face *magazine, where they serve as fashion editors on the Bulletin section.*

Contact Numbers: Photographers

Many thanks to the publications and photographers who allowed their work to be reproduced. Special thanks to Debbie Kirby, Kelly Worts, Sandra Scott, Fiona Foulgar, Katrina Christie, Rosee Laurence, Phil Bicker.

Page 43, top right
Anna Arnone
071-326 0164

Page 62, bottom centre
Bleddyn Butcher
071-790 9292

Page 19, top right
Page 23
Andrew Catlin
071-247 5580

Page 43, bottom left
Page 75
Page 77
Echoes
15 Newman St
London W1
071-436 4540

Page 43, top left
Echoes
(Jon Futrell)
15 Newman St
London W1
071-436 4540

Page 43, bottom right
Page 47
Page 63, bottom right
Chris George
21 Wellington Rd
Wanstead
London E11
071-735 1200 (ext 130)

Page 51
Julian Germain
38 Hermes Point
Chippenham Rd
London W9
071-494 0762

Page 49, bottom left
Page 50, top left, bottom right
Page 126
Patrick Harrison
4 Anerly Station Rd
Anerly
London SE20 8PT

Page 56
Page 57, top, centre and bottom
Tim Leighton-Boyce
24 St Albans House
176 Leighham Court Rd
London SW16 2RF
081-677 6301

Page 40, Page 65
Mark Lewis
15 rue Henry Monnier
Paris 75009 France
42 85 8966

Page 20/21
Page 68
Oliver Maxwell
Pager No. 0459 115770

Page 46, top and bottom
Leon Morris
56B Hawley Rd
London NW1
071-267 6959

Page 49, right
Matthew Naylor
071-639 4915
Pager: 081-884 3344
(No. A4095)

Page 43, top right
Page 57, top left, top right
Paul Sunman
Slam City Skates
128 Talbot Rd
London W11 1JA
071-221 7495
Fax: 071-221 1146

Page 32
Colin Thomas
Colin Thomas Photography
56 Whitfield St
London W1
071-637 4786

Page 36
Page 50, bottom left
Jeff Veitch
(*Echoes; The Face*)

Page 34
Echoes
(Lindsay Wesker)

Page 52, bottom
Andy Williams

Page 29
Steve Wright
0831-4020 75